Short Walks in the Lake District

Also by Bob Allen

On High Lakeland Fells Escape to the Dales
On Lower Lakeland Fells On Foot in Snowdonia
Walking the Ridges of Lakeland

SHORT WALKS
IN THE LAKE DISTRICT

60 Walks for Short Days,
Wet Days – and with the Family

Bob Allen

MICHAEL JOSEPH
London

MICHAEL JOSEPH LTD

Published by the Penguin Group
27 Wrights Lane, London W8 5TZ
Viking Penguin Inc., 375 Hudson Street, New York, New York 10014, USA
Penguin Books Australia Ltd, Ringwood, Victoria, Australia
Penguin Books Canada Ltd, 10 Alcorn Avenue, Toronto, Ontario, Canada M4V 3B2
Penguin Books (NZ) Ltd, 182–190 Wairau Road, Auckland 10, New Zealand

Penguin Books Ltd, Registered Offices: Harmondsworth, Middlesex, England

First published March 1994
Second impression April 1995

Typeset in Linotron 11 on 12pt Goudy Old Style by Goodfellow & Egan Ltd, Cambridge
Printed in Great Britain by Butler & Tanner Limited, Frome, Somerset

A CIP catalogue record for this book is available from the British Library

ISBN 0 7181 3694 2

Front cover photograph: *The village of Kentmere, with Kentmere Pike on the skyline*
Back cover photograph: *The author near Grasmere (©Jonathan Allen)*
Endpaper illustration: *Autumnal reflections in Yew Tree Tarn near Tarn Hows*
Introductory illustrations – on page 1: *The village of Seathwaite in the Duddon Valley, with Caw behind*
Page 2: *Kentmere village seen from the track up to Whiteside End*

CONTENTS

Introduction   7

Walks in the South-West

1. Great Langdale   11
2. Pike of Blisco and Blea Tarn   15
3. Little Langdale and Little Fell from Tilberthwaite   19
4. Blake Rigg and Hawk Rigg from Tilberthwaite   21
5. Boulder Valley and Levers Water from Haws Bank   25
6. Torver Back Common from Beckstones   29
7. The Beacon and Beacon Tarn from Beckstones   31
8. Torver High Common from near Torver   35
9. Woodland Fell and Wool Knott from near Torver   39
10. Blawith Knott and Tottlebank Height   43
11. Swinside Stone Circle   45
12. White Combe   49
13. Tarn Hill and Stickle Pike from near Ulpha   53
14. Park Head Road and Long Mire Beck   55
15. Caw and White Pike from Seathwaite   59
16. Tarn Beck and Fickle Steps   63
17. Seathwaite Tarn from the Duddon Valley   67
18. Harter Fell from Froth Pot   71
19. Buck Barrow to Devoke Water: a traverse   75
20. A Circuit of Devoke Water   77
21. Blea Tarn, Siney Tarn and the River Esk   81
22. The Stone Circles and Boat How from Boot   85
23. Eel Tarn and Stony Tarn from the Woolpack Inn   87
24. Green Crag and Low Birker Tarn   91
25. Yewbarrow from Overbeck Bridge   95
26. Nether Wasdale   99

Walks in the South-East

27. Scout Scar and Sizergh Castle   103
28. Cunswick Scar and Tarn   105
29. Lord's Lot from Crook   109
30. Carron Crag, Grizedale Forest   111
31. The Tarns of Tarn Hows from Coniston   115
32. Latterbarrow from Outgate   119
33. The Tarns of Claife Heights from Far Sawrey   121
34. Potter Tarn and the River Kent from Staveley   125
35. Skeggles Water and Longsleddale   129
36. The Head of Kentmere   131
37. Whiteside End and Kentmere Tarn   135
38. Lily Tarn on Loughrigg Fell from Rydal   137
39. Little Loughrigg and Loughrigg Fell   141
40. Sawrey's Wood and Fletcher's Wood   143
41. Megs Gill and Huntingstile from Grasmere   147

42.	Easedale Tarn	149
43.	Steel Fell and the Greenburn Skyline	153

Walks in the North

44.	Low Rigg and the Naddle Valley	157
45.	Cat Gill and Walla Crag, Borrowdale	161
46.	Falcon Crag and Ashness Bridge	165
47.	King's How and the Bowder Stone	167
48.	Tarn at Leaves and Bessyboot from Borrowdale	171
49.	High Spy from Grange	175
50.	Barrow and Newlands Beck from Braithwaite	179
51.	Barf and Lord's Seat	183
52.	Knott Rigg and Sail Beck from Newlands Hause	187
53.	Brackenthwaite Hows and Lanthwaite Wood	191
54.	Darling Fell and Low Fell, Loweswater	195
55.	Whitewater Dash and Great Calva	199
56.	Great Sca Fell	203
57.	Bowscale Fell and Tarn from Mungrisdale	207
58.	Scales Tarn and Souther Fell from Mungrisdale	211
59.	Mires Beck and Lanty's Tarn from Glenridding	215
60.	Caiston Glen and Red Screes	219
	Acknowledgements and Index	221

Caudalebeck Farm in Caiston Glen, looking towards Place Fell

INTRODUCTION

This book is an illustrated collection of sixty of the best short walks in the Lake District, all within the National Park. Nearly three-quarters of them are in the southern (south-west and south-east) part of it, simply because of the lie of the land; the walks in the northern sector, with a few exceptions, tend to rise to greater heights but have open and easy walking.

These walks cover just over 270 miles/435km and 54,000ft/16,459m in total, averaging just over 4½ miles/7.2km each, and with a height gain of just under 900ft/274m. All except one are 'rounds', returning to the start point. A few are still tough, gaining altitude quickly. Most are short but comparatively easy, walking over undulating land to some high-point or other objective. Whether a particular walk is suitable for your own requirements should be clearer from the full specifications. A number of them either start from a pub or have a pub near to hand at some point. Distances are not exact, simply calculated by running a map-measurer along the route on the map and the 'height gained' is the addition of the bits of uphill walking involved. The 'star rating' for the quality of the walk is completely subjective, three stars being for the best, but one star definitely does not mean that the walk is of no interest. To avoid confusion, reference is frequently made to points of

the compass as well as 'right' and 'left' etc, and to carry one, as well as the relevant OS map, will obviously be helpful.

Access: Below the level of the high land, in the valley bottoms within the intake fields, are those areas of land which are used for crop growing, forestry or, more likely, sheep or cattle grazing. While inside these areas all the walks in this book use either public rights of way which are marked on the relevant OS maps or permissive paths agreed by the Lake District National Park. These are indicated by gates or stiles at the relevant points and are usually signed as well. All walkers have a duty to stick to these access ways and ensure that gates are always closed. There is no necessity to climb over any walls except by a stile.

Maps: The OS maps, particularly the four superb Outdoor Leisure series at the 1:25 000 scale, are generally very good at showing these valley paths and for that reason walkers are strongly urged to carry them and use them. Where they are sometimes not so good is in showing the paths that walkers have developed through usage (the Harvey maps at the 1:40 000 scale are often clearer). This is because, although there are some exceptions, such as areas where there is grouse shooting or have specific conservation needs, there is freedom to walk on the higher

land, that above the level of cultivation. This freedom is probably greater here than in any other National Park in England or Wales, and long may it continue! The National Park managers and rangers are continually negotiating new access agreements with landowners and every walker and climber must be appreciative of what is being done in this respect.

In the unlikely event that, whilst using this guide book, any walker finds himself or herself on private land whose owner is not prepared to allow access, then he or she is probably lost! In such circumstances, the walker should apologise and request help; courteous negotiation is always the best way to resolve all these matters.

I hope the sketch maps will be clear enough not to need explanation, perhaps beyond mentioning that a single black line indicates a wall.

The red numbers on the three section maps refer to the Walk numbers. Each of these maps has a dotted line running across the map, indicating the areas covered by the OS 1:25 000 Outdoor Leisure maps:

Walks in the South-West: the northern area will be found on Map 6, South Western Area.

Walks in the South-East: the northern area will be found on Map 7, South Eastern Area.

Walks in the North: the southern area will be found on Maps 4 and 5, North Western and North Eastern Areas respectively.

Kelly Hall Tarn with the Coniston Fells beyond

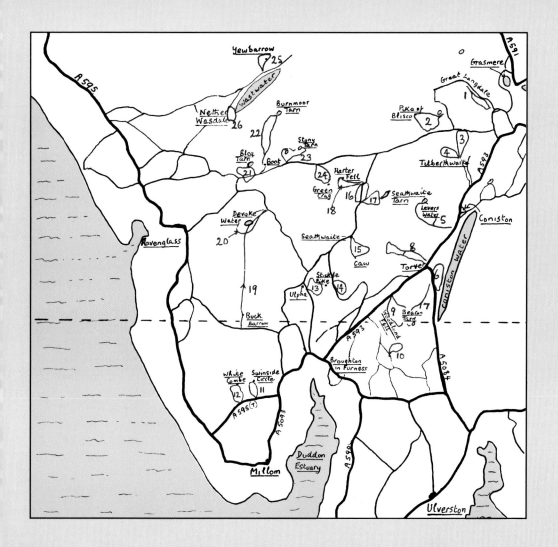

PART ONE

*Walks in the
South-West*

1. Great Langdale

Best Map: OS 1:25 000 Outdoor Leisure 6, South
    Western area

Distance: About 5¾ miles/9.2km

Highest elevation reached: About 425ft/130m

Height gained: About 200ft/61m

Star rating: * * *

Level of exertion: Low

Time for the round: About 3 hours

Terrain: All on clear paths; a few muddy or stony
    sections.

There was a time, only thirty-odd years ago, when Great Langdale didn't have a camp-site; walkers came up the valley in the bus from Ambleside and climbers dossed at Wall End Barn, at the foot of the steep road over to Little Langdale. Times have certainly changed. But, instead of joining the mad rush to the high fells, why not, for once, try a quiet alternative which also coincides for some of the distance with the Cumbrian Way.

The superb Langdale Pikes dominate the green valley bottom criss-crossed by walls and are the most outstanding feature, but not the only one, along much of this undulating but almost level walk. Pubs at the start and the halfway point may well enhance its pleasures, especially on a wet day.

Start from the main car park beside the Dungeon Ghyll New Hotel near the head of Great Langdale (grid ref 295064). Turn left down the valley road but then immediately right onto the farm track across Great Langdale Beck, to Side House. Beyond the yard, a footbridge and a turn down the valley lead to a gate, then a rising slope leads to another one through the main intake wall, built of rounded not flat stones. It is amazing how they hold together, but they do.

The path now stays outside this wall, below slopes colonised by bracken and juniper, descending then rising again, passing between stone walls and crossing ice-smoothed slabs, more of which can be seen on the left by a stand of oak trees. The smooth grey stone of these *roches moutonnées* looks remarkably like the backs of the sheep grazing nearby. There are fine views of the Langdale Pikes along here but these are now lost for a time as the path swings away from the river to reach the barn and cottage of Oak Howe, behind a knoll. Go right here and forward into Hag Wood with its mature oak and larch trees. As the trees thin out, the path joins a track from the old quarries leading to Baysbrown Farm.

*Great Langdale and the
Langdale Pikes from near
Oak Howe*

11

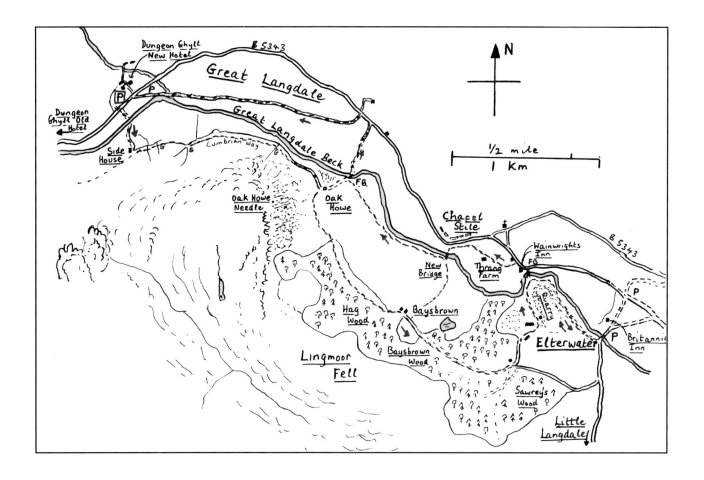

You could reduce the walk by 2 miles/3.2km if you took a signed path to Chapel Stile from just beyond the farm, but otherwise go ahead along the metalled track through Baysbrown Wood as far as the first dwelling on the left. This is Crossgates Cottage and from here a bridleway (sign) leads left to pass through Elterwater Quarries. It turns off the main track just before reaching a house, goes down a path leading through a cutting in a spoil-heap, to reach the Great Langdale Beck again. Either turn right and continue along the bank, shortly rising to a metalled track which leads into Elterwater and the Britannia Inn, or turn left across the footbridge to Wainwrights Inn.

Assuming you go into Elterwater: afterwards, retrace your steps to the footbridge crossing Great Langdale Beck to Wainwrights Inn. Turning left, a footpath will be found, beneath superb beech trees, just in front of the school in Chapel Stile. This leads past Thrang Farm, signed, to turn across the fine slate New Bridge to the south side of Great Langdale Beck again. The path now goes along the river's embankment, then cuts across a bend to a solid footbridge (financed by the Friends of the Lake District) just north-east of Oak Howe. This leads to the road again but you only use it for fifty or so paces before turning off it and down a track signed 'Footpath Dungeon Ghyll'. This leads, almost as straight as an arrow, and with more grand views up Stickle Ghyll to Pavey Ark, back to the car park.

Looking down Great Langdale from near Oak Howe

2. Pike of Blisco and Blea Tarn

Best Map: OS 1:25 000 Outdoor Leisure 6, South Western area

Distance: About 4½ miles/7.2km

Highest elevation reached: 2313ft/705m

Height gained: About 1650ft/503m

Star rating: * *

Level of exertion: Fairly high

Time for the round: About 3 hours

Terrain: Fairly good fell paths on the ascent; mostly on grass over open fell on the descent and some boggy bits on the last stretch.

Pike of Blisco (also known as Pike o' Blisco) is a fine, conical and almost isolated peak at the head of Great Langdale but one which is often ignored by fellwalkers intent on traversing Crinkle Crags and Bowfell. Blea Tarn, near its foot, in its particular setting, is one of the loveliest in the Lake District. This walk visits them both, giving an excellent short round.

Start from the National Trust car park, surrounded by conifers and overlooked by the crags of Blake Rigg, on the road that links Little Langdale with Great Langdale, just east of Blea Tarn (grid ref 295043). A path leads to the south end of the tarn, giving a classic view over its waters to the jutting Langdale Pikes, and then turns north along the west bank. This path used to burrow through overgrown rhododendrons but the National Trust have made a good job of cutting them back, improving both the views and the footing. This path carries on round the toe of the long ridge thrown down to the north by Blake Rigg and reaches the road, then a short walk down this reveals a path turning back up Redacre Gill, which is the direction needed. But rather than lose height, before reaching the road, turn uphill instead on a grassy path through bracken leading to an obvious little col on the ridge. There are gaps in the wall here and a traversing path leads to a connection with the main one, which now goes up a wide tongue of land between the main subsidiary gills. This rises at what I should describe as an easy angle; what is 'easy' here depends on how fit you are. Nearing the top of the tongue, the path deteriorates into a little river of scree but emerges onto easier-angled land with Pike of Blisco visible ahead. Peaty ground now alternates with almost horizontal rock slabs although, as height is gained,

On the summit of Pike of Blisco, with Crinkle Crags and Bowfell beyond

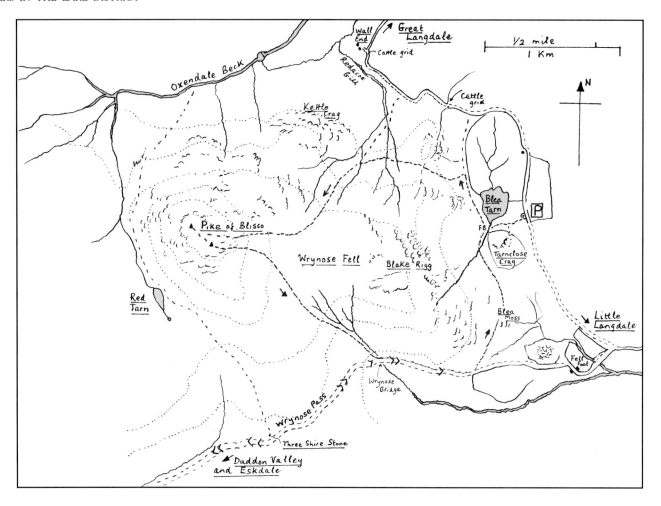

the slabs become little rock walls and ledges, the biggest of these being surmounted by an easy gully. A final passage over rocks and grass leads to a rocky twin summit with a cairn on each. The view from the most westerly cairn, overlooking Oxendale, is to Crinkle Crags and Bowfell and makes all the effort worth while.

From the other cairn, descend over rocky ground to the south-east; the path is very faint and soon lost but the line of descent, into a wide depression south of the rocky top of Blake Rigg, is over grass and obvious enough. Lower down, a few cairns appear and you find yourself (although I presume you were not lost) going along the bank of one of the streams which merge to form the Wrynose Beck, reaching the Wrynose Pass at, you'd never guess, Wrynose Bridge.

Walk down the unfenced road, but only until the first wall appears on the right-hand side (grid ref 292032). From here a path leads over boggy ground and then onto firm ground, contouring round to Blea Tarn again.

On this very last bit of the walk, as you again pass the tarn and are tempted to take yet another photograph (I have myself taken scores from here over the years), it is well worth making a very short diversion to the top of Tarnclose Crag, overlooking this enchanting landscape, for a different view. There is a ladderstile over the wall on the right, placed there for the purpose.

Blea Tarn and the Langdale Pikes from Tarnclose Crag

3. Little Langdale and Little Fell from Tilberthwaite

Best Map: OS 1:25 000 Outdoor Leisure 6, South
      Western area

Distance: About 5 miles/8km

Highest elevation reached: About 720ft/219m

Height gained: About 450ft/137m

Star rating: * * *

Level of exertion: Low

Time for the round: About 3 hours

Terrain: All on good tracks or paths.

Several of our friends, when staying with us in the Lake District, have asked, when I have proposed a short walk rather than a harder and higher tramp on the big hills, 'Can we stop at a pub at lunch time?' – which will also tell you something about our friends! For a short, wet or hot day (or any other when you don't feel like putting out your best effort), it isn't such a bad idea. So I deliberately looked for some walks that would include this requirement. This is one of them, for the halfway point on this very interesting and most varied walk is the Three Shires

Inn in Little Langdale, where there is always a hospitable welcome.

Start from the car park at Tilberthwaite Gill (grid ref 307010), reached from the A593 Skelwith Bridge to Coniston road. The metalled track continues to the farms of Low and High Tilberthwaite and from this latter a cart track (the one on the left) winds uphill through oak woods to the top of a rise, well above the old slate quarries in the woods below. After two gates, the track reaches its highest point, with Lingmoor Fell seen directly ahead the other side of Little Langdale with its tarn; the path then descends to join another track almost at the base of the slope. Here turn back sharp right (east) and go down a walled lane passing High Hall Garth and then Low Hall Garth (a climbing club hut), to reach a gate and stile on the left. The path from here leads directly to the River Brathay, which is crossed by the charming Slater Bridge; then, at a gap in the wall, turn off the main path onto another going north-east. A little ramble across sloping pastures quickly leads to a metalled lane and, at the junction just beyond, turn right (east) to reach the Three Shires Inn.

Suitably fortified, walk east along the road past Wilson Place Farm to find a signed footpath on the right. This slopes down a meadow to a footbridge

In Little Langdale: the River Brathay near the Three Shires Inn

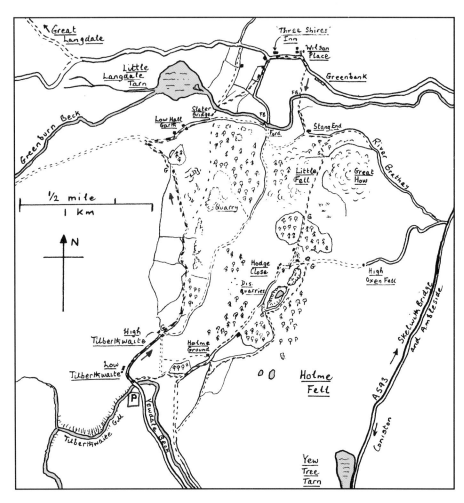

across the River Brathay again (which, for those who may have over-indulged at lunch time, has two handrails). The path leads up to the farm at Stang End. Turn left here along the tarmac but in two hundred paces look for a signed footpath on the right, heading south-west to a stile, beyond which it leads up onto a shoulder of Little Fell. Some delightful open country follows, until a gate into a wood is reached, and then a broader track. At a fork bear left, to meet another track with a stone shed on the corner.

From here a path winds down into the depths of the Hodge Close Quarries, leading through an archway to an iron platform just above the water which fills the bottom of the enormous quarry hole beyond. Divers told me that the water goes down a further 115ft/35m and the many underwater passages have notices to warn of the fate that may await (and has claimed) unlucky ones.

Returning to the track, turn eastwards and then right (south) at a gate opposite a little pond, when a green path leads through woodland, skirting the upper edge of the quarries to reach a gate and track at the south end of the main quarry. A broad path continues southwards through woods, then winds downhill to join one rising from the buildings of Holme Ground seen below. Turn sharp right to the gate leading onto the metalled road here and then left down the road for a further hundred paces or so beyond Holme Ground as far as a footpath sign on the right. From here a track leads into the woods and a signed footpath takes you directly back to the river bank and the car park.

4. Blake Rigg and Hawk Rigg from Tilberthwaite

Best Map: OS 1:25 000 Outdoor Leisure 6, South Western area

Distance: About 2½ miles/4km

Highest elevation reached: About 1345ft/410m

Height gained: About 1000ft/305m

Star rating: * * *

Level of exertion: Medium

Time for the round: About 2 hours

Terrain: Good paths, although rougher and steeper on the descent and return.

This short walk is a microcosm of much of what is best about fellwalking in the Lake District; a steady climb to a high point, some lovely gill scenery, fine tree-clad crags and fellsides, tumbling waters and some superb views. And all packed into little more than two miles.

Start from the good car park at the foot of Tilberthwaite Gill (grid ref 307010) reached from the A593 Skelwith Bridge to Coniston road. From here, continue to Low Tilberthwaite Farm; at the entrance to the yard, look for a sign 'Footpath to Wetherlam', then set off up a broad track swinging uphill behind the farm. After only 150 paces or so, the track continues to the old quarries of High Fell but a finger-post points you to the south-west, the path leading to a ford across a little beck, with a gate and stile facing you in the wall opposite. Beyond the stile, a good track slants up the fellside, passing a fenced-off mine-shaft, and running parallel to Tilberthwaite Gill on the left. Soon passing the point where a little footpath goes down to the steep, wooded ravine below – which is quite spectacular in autumn or after heavy rain – the track continues round the rocky corner ahead, turning north opposite some fenced-off shafts, a stone ruin and some mine spoil tips.

Passing below some fine little crags on Blake Rigg (not to be confused with the better-known fell of the same name above Blea Tarn in Little Langdale), the path continues to reach a large cairn and remains of a stone hut next to a mine adit, before curving round to the left (west) beneath more steep little crags on Hawk Rigg, on the right, with Wetherlam towering above the boggy depression on the left. Almost all other walkers will continue on the level here, on the main path round the upper part of the depression and heading for the higher fells, but turn uphill at the

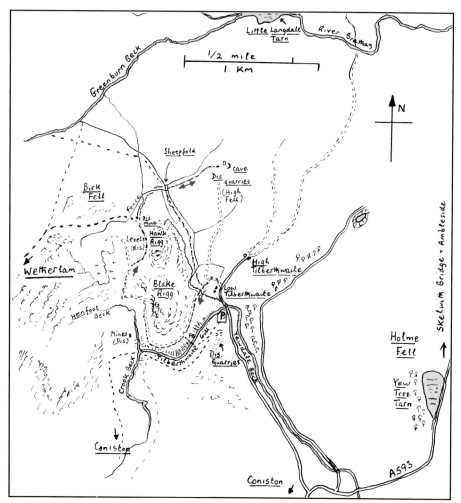

cairn and derelict hut, leaving the main path and almost immediately passing the rotting timbers of another fenced-off mine shaft. This fainter path climbs to a little col just to the north of Hawk Rigg (and the highest point of the walk) where there are some superb views to Helvellyn and the Langdale Pikes in particular.

The slope on the other side leads down a little wet valley to a fence and stile and then, curving downhill beside the fence to the east, you reach a little sheepfold at a junction of walls (grid ref 302018), where you join the main footpath from Greenburn to Tilberthwaite. The fellsides just to the east of the sheepfold are the site of numerous small disused slate quarries, and an impressive one is easily reached by going through the sheepfold and following the wall uphill to the north-east. Over a slight rise is a roofless building, slate spoil and a huge, square-cut, black-mouthed hole, like a cave. But don't wander any further; the old High Fell quarries are being worked again and you could risk being blown to kingdom come.

From the sheepfold, the path leads south-east down an almost level narrow valley with a wall on the left, then starts to descend quite steeply beside a delightful ravine adorned with larches. Descend over little rock outcrops, then a stile crosses a transverse wall and a last little bit of grassy path leads down to the little ford where the outward path is rejoined.

The Langdale Pikes seen from Hawk Rigg above Tilberthwaite

5. Boulder Valley and Levers Water from Haws Bank

Best Map: OS 1: 25 000 Outdoor Leisure 6, South Western area

Distance: About 5 miles/8km

Highest elevation reached: About 1400ft/427m

Height gained: About 1130ft/344m

Star rating: * *

Level of exertion: Low/medium

Time for the round: About 3 hours

Terrain: On good paths and tracks.

Levers Water lies in a cirque of high fells which for centuries were mined for copper and other ores and are still quarried for slate. The traces of the industrial past seen on this walk add greatly to its interest.

Preferably start from Haws Bank, a little south of Coniston on the A593 and park near the phone box just past the church (grid ref 299967). (If this is not possible, use the Old Station car park in Coniston (grid ref 301975) and then walk along the grassy former railway to Haws Bank.) Walk uphill beside the church, under the old railway line, turn right and follow the tarmac past a few houses and then uphill beside the Shelt Beck (not named on the OS map) to a gate. Still beside the beck, a rougher track, becoming a path as the lane ends, crosses the stream and rises across a field to the main intake wall where there are two gates side by side.

Turn right (WNW) here and follow a path beside the wall towards the scarred slopes of Coniston Old Man, now seen ahead. Over a slight rise, the path passes the point where cars are often parked at the metalled end of the 'Walna Scar Road' and continues ahead, now on a broad gravel track. This rises to a hause on a low ridge, with a rocky high point, The Bell. On this hause the tracks diverge; take the one going forward (north-west), ending below slate spoil-tips but continuing as a footpath. Soon passing a huge boulder, the 'Pudding Stone', cross Low Water Beck by a footbridge and then climb a tongue of rock and grass at the edge of 'Boulder Valley', named from the vast numbers of rocks that have fallen into it from Brim Fell above.

Reaching the top of the tongue, where there are several deep rifts with spoil heaps beside them, Levers Water comes into view below, surrounded by a ring of high rocky fellsides. Just recently, about a century after work there ceased, one of the old mines was

Levers Water, with a cloud-covered Great How Crags

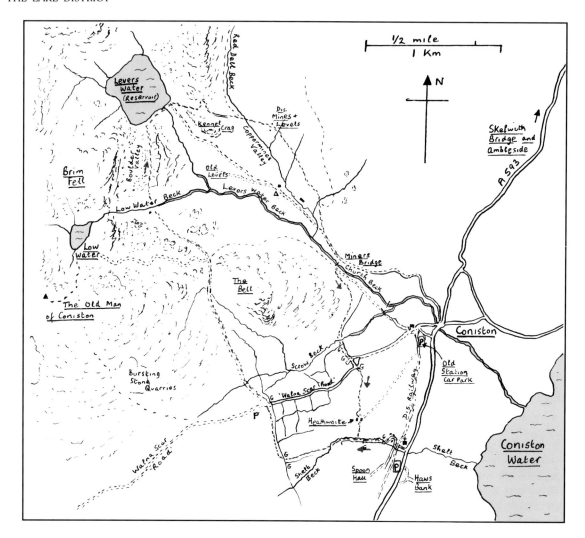

re-discovered, with a tunnel going right underneath the reservoir. Astonishingly, the researchers found the legendary oak plug sealing the bottom of Levers Water still to be in place. Cross the grassy top of the dam, then take a slightly rising grass path going south-east to cross the little ridge just above Kennel Crag. This path curves round to a former mine entrance, then more steeply downhill on the stony top of a man-made incline ending near a deep pit or slot which would once have contained a winding-wheel. The path beyond crosses Red Dell Beck to two towers from which ran hausers to a giant pump-engine in a tunnel which used to drain the copper-mine workings.

A grassy track now slants south-east, above the hearths and tips in the valley bottom where ores were once smelted, to where streams converge, thunder suddenly down a gorge and become Church Beck. Turn across the stone-arched Miners Bridge but (unless parked in Coniston, in which case just continue downhill) leave the main track immediately for a path rising across the fellside ahead. This soon crosses Scrow Beck by a footbridge and then reaches the Walna Scar Road. Leave this almost immediately along another track to a gate ahead, and where a green track leads south across fields to the farm at Heathwaite. From here a path is signed across more fields to connect with the rough track up Shelt Gill, where the outward route is rejoined.

Church Beck, Coniston

27

6. Torver Back Common from Beckstones

Best Map: OS 1:25 000 Outdoor Leisure 6, South Western area

Distance: About 3½ miles/5.6km

Highest elevation reached: About 470ft/143m

Height gained: About 200ft/61m

Star rating: * *

Time for the round: About 2 hours

Level of exertion: Low

Terrain: Almost all on pleasant grassy paths.

This easy ramble over an open common with a return alongside Coniston Water gives a delightful short walk with some attractive views. It is all over National Park Access Land and visitors have taken advantage of this and have added to the trods and paths created by sheep. The walk described is consequently one of several variations that are possible here.

Turn off the A593 at Torver, about 2½ miles/4km south of Coniston, and onto the A5084 (signed for Ulverston). In about 1 mile/1.6km you reach the hamlet of Beckstones, where there is a garage (Land-Rover specialists) on a bend in the road (grid ref 287932). You can park almost opposite on some open ground. A track east of the garage leads to a gate and sign 'Torver Commons' and the path beyond quickly discloses the tiny Kelly Hall Tarn, a good viewpoint for the Coniston Fells although, like the watched pot that never boils, it is amazing how many visits one may need to make to get a reasonable photograph of them. Continuing ahead, curving north-east, the grassy path passes a second tarn in the reedy depression of Long Moss, then ambles along over undulating land which is wrinkled and folded, with green rides like the finest lawn amongst the bracken and with rowans and juniper bushes scattered everywhere. Over a rise, Coniston Water comes into view, then there is a descent to an area where juniper bushes crowd thickly on the path and you reach a wooded gill. A path does continue down the gill, burrowing into the trees and junipers and leading down to the shore of Coniston Water, but the open views are lost and this variation curtails the walk too quickly. I therefore suggest that it is better to cross the beck here and follow round the side of the wall beyond onto open land at a higher level than the gill. There are several faint tracks here but the clearest continues round a grassy shoulder to join a track in a second gill

Long Moss Tarn, and a glimpse of Coniston Water

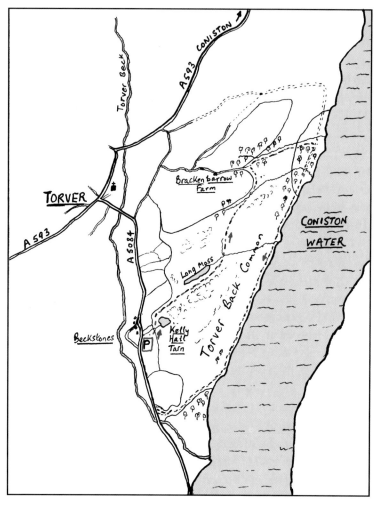

and which, if followed to the left (west), would lead to Brackenborrow Farm. Instead, turn right (north-east) downhill, on a good track leading through more woods of crack-willow, birch and oak to reach more open glades and a view of Coniston Water ahead. This time, it is only a short distance away and easily reached.

Turn south here along the lakeside and enjoy a delightful stroll through avenues of fine trees for a little way until the broad track narrows to a path and you cross a little stream via stones. Now the wood thins out, the land rises a little more steeply on the right and the path is forced almost to the water's edge as it alternately passes across more open land followed by narrow belts of woodland. It stays easy underfoot and although the view doesn't change much for a while you may be lucky and spot the steam-driven iron boat, the *Gondola*, chugging up and down the lake on its pleasure-cruises. Or you may try to spot the sites of ancient bloomeries, of which there were apparently several examples along here, where the trees were slowly burned to form charcoal which was then used in smelting iron ore.

When you reach a bench and a boatshed, the path turns uphill again beside a wall enclosing wooded parkland. It quickly reaches a gate and stile at a wire fence, then joins a farm track which leads round a grassy shoulder to meet the main road just five minutes walk from the car park. As you probably didn't fail to notice, Torver has two inns, just up the road . . .

7. The Beacon and Beacon Tarn from Beckstones

Best Map: OS 1:25 000 Outdoor Leisure 6, South
  Western area

Distance: About 5 miles/8km

Highest elevation reached: 837ft/255m

Height gained: About 600ft/183m

Star rating: **/***

Level of exertion: Medium

Time for the round: About 2½ hours

Terrain: A mixture of good paths on grass, rougher
  ones on rockier ground and farm tracks.

Despite their low elevation, the Blawith Fells to the south-west of Coniston Water are remarkably rugged, giving splendid walking more akin to that on much higher land. This walk is a good example.

Before you start looking for it, however, you will not find the name 'Beacon Fell' on the OS maps, only a spot height of 255m on one particular point of the Blawith Fells (which the OS do name) and something marked 'Beacon' next to it (grid ref 278907). There can surely be no doubt but that this beacon is on Beacon Fell, a ridge rising to a clearly defined rocky high point and with an almost conical shape recognizable from many surrounding places. It is an outstanding little summit and fellwalkers generally and rightly distinguish it by the name 'Beacon Fell' even though the OS haven't got around to that so far; I certainly cannot help calling it this.

The route chosen avoids the more normal tarmac approach to Beacon Fell from the Brown Howe picnic area beside Coniston Water to give increased interest and variety. There is a Land-Rover garage at Beckstones, a hamlet 1 mile/1.6km south of Torver on the A5084. Some 300 yds/275m south of the garage, about six cars can park on the side of the road (grid ref 288927) at a point where you can look to the south-west, directly up an enchanting side valley drained by Mere Beck. The signed footpath ('Torver Commons') leads down to a footbridge (not stepping-stones as on the OS map) across Torver Beck and then rises gently up this valley through ash trees, gorse and juniper onto slightly higher land. The old reservoir is out of sight unless you turn off the main path up the course of a little stream flowing from it.

A line of telegraph poles can now be seen heading south towards the distinctive conical shape of what you realize from its shape must be Beacon Fell and, having forded the tiny Mere Beck, the path joins a

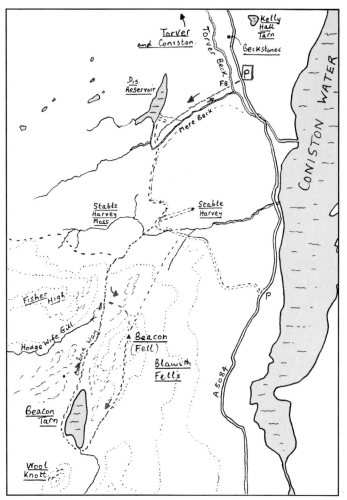

better track heading in the same direction. Skirting a boggy basin, Stable Harvey Moss, on its east side, this track reaches an unfenced but metalled road, the drive to Stable Harvey (Farm). Turn right (south-west) along this but leave it again in about 50 paces and follow another path curving upwards into a defile on the west side of Beacon Fell (part of the Cumbria Way). The path leads up this to reach a boggy section with several small reedy tarns. From here, turn left on grassy tracks and simply make for the high land ahead, soon reaching the large cairn, the beacon on Beacon Fell. This is a marvellous viewpoint, giving a complete panorama around the compass as far as Fairfield, Black Combe and, of course, the Coniston fells which dominate the view.

The one thing you cannot see is Beacon Tarn. For this you must go a little further south along paths through the heather on this craggy little ridge and then it comes into view, a surprisingly large sheet of water for these miniature fells, triangular in shape and with little heather-covered crags on its eastern side. A good path leads down to its shore, crosses the outflow, rounds its margin, passes a pretty little coppice of trees on the west bank and then rises to a col just to the west of the beacon. Here you are in the boggy depression which is the source of Strands Beck flowing down Hodge Wife Gill to the south-west and should reverse what remains of the approach walk back to the car park.

Beacon Tarn and Wool Knott from Beacon Fell

8. Torver High Common from near Torver

Best Map: OS 1:25 000 Outdoor Leisure 6, South Western area

Distance: About 5½ miles/8.8km; or 3½ miles/5.6km for shorter version

Highest elevation reached: 2037ft/621m or about 990ft/302m for shorter version

Height gained: About 1690ft/515m or 630ft/192m for shorter version

Star rating: * *

Level of exertion: Longer route – medium/high; shorter route – fairly low

Time for the round: Longer route – about 3½ hours; shorter route – about 2 hours

Terrain: Good paths and tracks on the ascent; open fell for the descent to Torver Bottom; path boggy in places on return journey.

Torver High Common is south of the quarry-scarred breast of The Old Man of Coniston, an apparently featureless area overlooked by walkers heading for the Dow Crag circuit, but it is well worth visiting. The shorter walk avoids around 1000ft/305m of ascent and 2 miles/3.2km of distance.

Park beside the A593 south of Coniston on the elbow of the road just north of Torver (grid ref 285945) or on a layby by the road sign for 'Torver' (going south) at grid ref 288947. Now walk north-east to turn off the main road into the hamlet of Little Arrow. From here a path rises through gorse, bracken and a few trees to a gate, then beside a wall, and over a little rise to gain a splendid view of Dow Crag seen beyond the wooded gill of Torver Beck on the left. Leading forward, nearer the beck now, the path passes between the spoil-tips of some old quarries and then circles a huge flooded quarry crater, with a waterfall pouring into it which, for walkers in the Yorkshire Dales, will be highly reminiscent of Hull Pot.

A path on grass now shadows the beck again, soon joining the much broader track of the Walna Scar Road. Multi-coloured mountain-bikers use this bridle-way nowadays as well as walkers, insisting that it is easier on the downhill. It may be true, on a reasonable surface, but I'm not yet convinced that the wheels are as good as shanks's pony for going uphill on a rough track like this. For the shorter walk you would not go so far but cross the beck and head south-west alongside a wall leading to the old workings at Torver Bottom. For the longer route, turn left (west) along the 'road', over the little packhorse bridge and then fairly steeply upwards below more old workings on the

Coniston Old Man seen from Ash Gill Beck

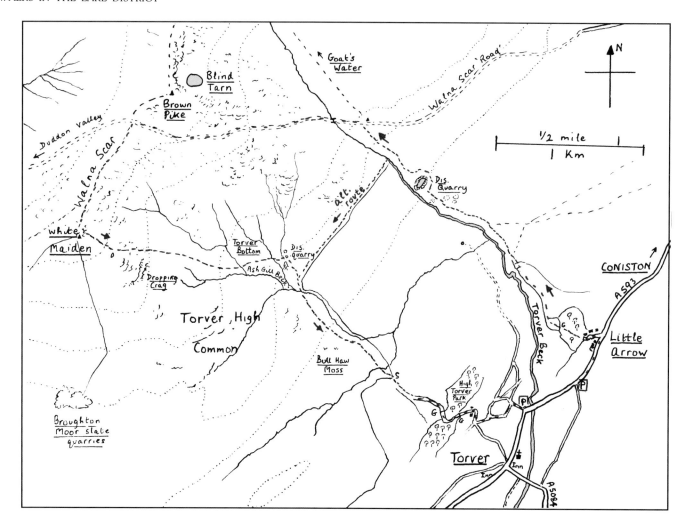

shoulder of Brown Pike. You pass a tiny roofed stone shelter, into which you can just about squeeze two people for a bite of lunch out of the wind.

The top of the ridge, the hause, is just a little further. From here the main track continues downhill to the Duddon Valley, a well-used one turns right up the ridge to Brown Pike and a very faint one goes south-west out along the grassy edge of Walna Scar. Even this faint path swings away from the few spiky rocks, a tumbledown cairn and remnants of wall on top of White Maiden, but it is a quiet spot well away from the well-worn track over the Dow Crag ridge top. Here you may lie undisturbed, listen to the skylarks, pick out the yachts on Coniston Water far below and just watch the world go by for a while before beginning the descent. Head ESE towards the basin of Ash Gill Beck, using the occasional sheep track, and go easily down a broad, grassy and occasionally rocky ridge. Pass a tiny tarn (not shown on the map) and skirt rock buttresses before reaching the old quarrying area here, just east of Torver Bottom: this is where the shorter route re-joins. Now follow the path down beside Ash Gill Beck.

There are a few squelchy moments while crossing some evil boggy bits on the flat Bull Haw Moss, but then a gate, stile and arrow sign point down a gill towards the woods of High Torver Park, seen ahead. A semi-sunken lane (a stream-bed in wet weather) leads to a gate and an unmistakable walled lane through a belt of woodland to emerge and pass between a house and a barn. Swing right here and

ahead can be seen Torver Church; nearby are two pubs. Alternatively, if you bear left, you will find the way easily to the main road at the 'elbow', the first of the suggested parking places.

The disused quarry near the head of Torver Beck

9. Woodland Fell and Wool Knott from near Torver

Best Maps: OS 1:25 000 Outdoor Leisure 6, South
Western area *plus* Pathfinder 626 Broughton
in Furness and Newby Bridge (both needed).
Alternatively, use OS 1:50 000 Landranger 96
Barrow-in-Furness

Distance: About 6 miles/9.6km

Highest elevation reached: About 728ft/222m

Height gained: About 640ft/195m

Star rating: * *

Level of exertion: Medium

Time for the round: About 3½ hours

Terrain: On grassy tracks and paths, mostly
through bracken and heather.

South-east of the main A593 from Torver to
Broughton in Furness is an area of little noticed
but inviting wild fells, well worth visiting. Parking for
a couple of cars is possible on the roadside opposite
Troughton Hall Farm (grid ref 257918), about two
miles south-west of Torver. From here, there is a good
view across the wide valley to a prominent cairn on
Yew Bank seen above the screes of Pool Scar. Also
easily seen from the car park, rising from the valley
bottom towards Pool Scar, is a tempting wide grassy
track leading to a shoulder and a mysterious landscape
beyond with little rocky tops emerging from it. There
is in fact a network of paths and tracks here which are
obvious in winter; they are not so clear in summer
when the bracken is high but are still detectable.
Head towards Pool Scar down the field (public footpath sign) to a ladder-stile and onto the level green
way of an old railway. Go left, but only for twenty
paces, then turn downhill again on a path through
trees (yellow arrow) to a footbridge across the beck,
then over a stile into a grassy walled lane. Turn right
here (south) and after two gates reach the green track
seen from the parking place, which does indeed rise to
a hause just south of Pool Scar.

The tall high cairn on Yew Bank is just above, is
easily visited and is a good viewpoint, but then return
to the track which descends towards a broad basin and
starts swinging south-west. Leave it for a less well-
defined one rising to the south, keeping outside the
intake wall surrounding the farm of Climb Stile and
heading for the top edge of a wood beyond. When the
wall round the wood turns south-west, cross a little
stream and continue up the slope beyond to join a
well-used green track (just a short way east of Green
Moor). This track rises to the east alongside Wood-

*To Black Combe from
Bell Knott*

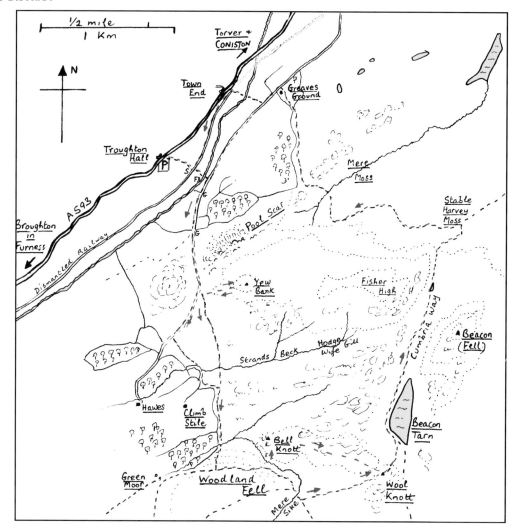

land Fell to a boggy basin drained by Mere Sike, and the little eminence of Bell Knott, crowned by two slender rowan trees, is just to the north across the beck and easily reached. Bell Knott is the blunt end of a broad ridge which terminates in twin rocky summits: these crown Wool Knott which is reached either along the heathery ridge or by a grassy path through the bracken at a lower level. An unexpected view of Beacon Tarn is revealed from its rocky little summit.

A good grassy path now leads down to pass the west side of the tarn and then rises to a col to the left (west) side of Beacon Fell, strangely not named as such by the OS although the beacon on the summit is marked. A level boggy basin follows, then the path descends to the broad area of Stable Harvey Moss. Here you turn west. The initially obvious path soon becomes confused by sheep tracks, but keep going west on the drier land to reach the well-defined shallow valley of Mere Moss. Cross this at its south-west end to a notch in the ridge beyond, then head north beside the wall marking the National Park Access Land. The path improves as Greaves Ground is reached. A signed path leads to a tarmac drive, then another path leads down the field to the west to meet the A593 at Town End. Don't take the road; it's much better to turn left along the adjacent green track of the old railway again to reach the ladder-stile that was used on the outward journey. A gentle climb up the slope beyond leads back to the car.

Looking north to the Coniston Fells from just below Pool Scar

10. Blawith Knott and Tottlebank Height

Best Maps: OS 1:25 000 Pathfinder 626 Broughton
in Furness and Newby Bridge; or
OS 1:50 000 Landranger 96 Barrow-in-Furness

Distance: About 2½ miles/4km

Highest elevation reached: About 810ft/247m

Height gained: About 500ft/152m

Star rating: *

Level of exertion: Low

Time for the round: About 1 hour

Terrain: Good path to Blawith Knott, a rougher
descent, then a good track.

The late Alfred Wainwright wrote in his *Outlying Fells of Lakeland* that anyone who couldn't manage to get to the top of Gummer's How should hang their boots up for good. The ascent of Blawith Knott could probably fit into the same category but, like Gummer's How, it is a fine viewpoint. However, you don't have to be in the earlier stages of senility, your knees creaking or your hip twingeing to enjoy this little walk. For those who aren't knackered but just hopelessly unfit, anything like this will still be a challenge.

Blawith Knott is another distinctive top amongst the fairly low but wild Furness fells lying between the A593 and the A5084 south of Torver and has the incomparable advantage of being visible and easily attained from the unfenced fell road over Subberthwaite Common. Just beyond its highest point on the north side, the road is crossed by a public bridleway, with a finger-post sign on the junction marked for Tottlebank on one side and for the hamlet of Fell Gate on the other.

Just south of the junction, and just beyond the highest point reached by the road, there is parking for about a dozen cars (grid ref 257878). From here, walk down the road to the junction and take the obvious path (not the bridleway) climbing to the north-east up the broad ridge of grass and bracken, with occasional outcropping rocks, to attain the cairn on top of Blawith Knott. A fine panorama is now visible, with the Blawith fells, the distant Scafells and the high Coniston fells all displayed.

As I sat by the cairn here and the sheep moved away, presumably because they realized my two little dogs would already have had any of my lunch that I was prepared to hand over, I watched an amazing

The Scafells and Caw seen from Blawith Knott

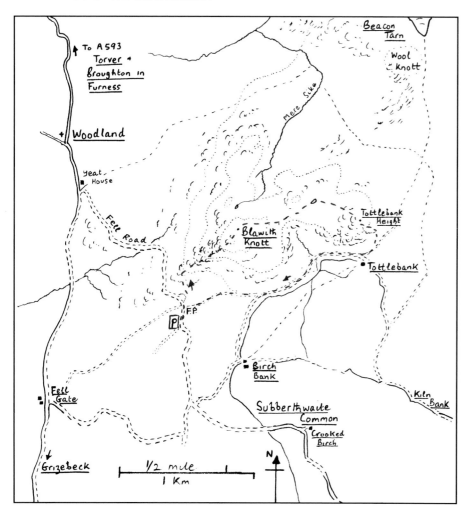

aerial spectacle that I have only ever seen once before and that was high in Burtness Comb, Buttermere. A hawk, presumably a peregrine, flying high in the sky, stooped at a pigeon but, as above Buttermere, it failed to strike cleanly. The pigeon staggered in the air and there was a puff of white feathers but the foiled raptor could not recover in time for a second attempt and the pigeon escaped. I believe that such attacks on racing pigeons are increasingly common as peregrines are a protected species and their numbers are now increasing rapidly.

To the east another cairn is visible in the near distance, on Tottlebank Height. A faint path undulates along the height of land towards it, linking little rocky high points in the heather and bracken on the way and passing a shallow tarn (often dry) just before reaching it. As a viewpoint, it can hardly be much different from Blawith Knott but there is a new glimpse of Coniston Water and, on a clear day, the eye can reach as far as the distant Howgill Fells the other side of the M6.

Sheep trods down the bracken-covered slopes to the east quickly lead to a grassy path heading generally south-west and descending to Tottlebank Farm. A tarmac track ends here and its continuation, a rough cart track leading west, is part of the bridleway leading back to the fell road; when this track veers off left (towards Birch Bank) continue straight ahead and a less used track soon completes the little circuit. Those who are exhausted had better take up some serious exercise to get in better shape.

11. Swinside Stone Circle

Best Maps: OS 1:25 000 Pathfinder 625 Broughton
in Furness; or
OS 1:50 000 Landranger 96 Barrow-in-Furness

Distance: About 3½ miles/5.6km

Highest elevation reached: About 675ft/206m

Height gained: About 350ft/107m

Star rating: *

Level of exertion: Low

Time for the round: About 2 hrs

Terrain: Firm cart tracks, then some rougher paths
on the return.

In my experience, the prehistoric stone circle at
Swinside, to the north-east of Black Combe and
White Combe, is the finest in the Lake District after
the famous one at Castlerigg, near Keswick. If such
extraordinary monuments are simply a heap of old
stones to you, this short walk will have little interest;
if, on the other hand, they seem charged with mystery
and set your imagination alight as you wonder at their
purpose, it will be a walk full of anticipation which
will render the rather dull approach walk endurable.
The return is much better.

The A5093 turns off to Millom from the A595 at
Hallthwaites, but the turn-off to the hamlet of
Broadgate is reached north of this, about 1 mile/
1.6km before the junction. Approaching from the
east, turn right onto the now by-passed old main road
(grid ref 181865) which always provides convenient
parking.

Walk up the metalled road through the quiet
hamlet of Broadgate, turning left at a fork just before
the house called Crag Hall onto a rough cart-track
(signed 'Public Bridleway Swinside Stone Circle and
Thwaites Fell'.) This leads quickly to the east of
Knott Hill to the farm at Swinside and the stone
circle will be found just south of the farm.

The circle is about 30 paces in diameter and 24 of
its 50 stones are standing with some of the remainder
leaning. As is so often the case, it is situated in a
cirque of fine fells with the summit of Dow Crag being
clearly visible; due north, the rounded hill with the
prominent cairn is Whitfell.

Leaving the stones, go through the gate in the wall
just south of them and, as the farm track heads back
south-east, walk due south across gently rising rough
pasture (not much sign of the path yet) making for the
right of the shoulder on Knott Hill, seen clearly

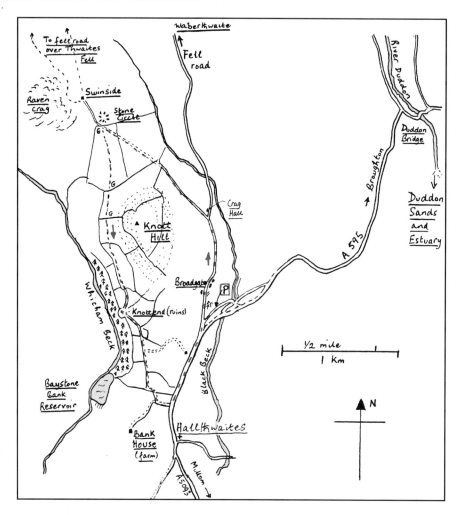

ahead. After a gate and a stile, Barrow and Isle of Walney come into view to seaward, Black Combe and White Combe are both revealed and conifers fringe the Whicham Beck in the near foreground. A path soon develops, looks as if it will turn into a regular track but then disappears into gorse and bracken. The direction alongside the nearby wall is obvious enough, however, and a little-used tractor-track soon appears and leads into an overgrown walled lane conducting you down to the ruins of Knottend gently crumbling away within a little enclosure colonized by sycamores and a solitary pear tree.

A gate out of the enclosure leads into another walled lane going south but it soon turns into more open fields. Ignore the tractor-track swinging away to the left and, comforted by little yellow arrows on posts, follow them easily until you reach the main road near Bank House Farm. I write 'easily' with reservation because when I crossed these fields my two little dogs were charged repeatedly by a herd of curious young bullocks. Since I was also in the firing-line I was pretty unnerved myself and only by flapping my arms at them could I keep them at bay. I gained ground slowly towards the cattle-grid but the last fifty paces turned to a rout as I grabbed both dogs, threw them across the grid and leapt across it myself. What a pantomime!

Turn left (north-east) up the road and you are quickly back at the car.

Swinside Stone Circle, with the Coniston Fells in the distance

12. White Combe

Best Maps: OS 1:25 000 Pathfinder 625 Broughton
in Furness; or
OS 1:50 000 Landranger 96 Barrow-in-Furness

Distance: About 4 miles/6.4km

Highest elevation reached: About 1400ft/427m

Height gained: About 1240ft/378m

Star rating: */**

Level of exertion: Medium plus

Time for the round: 3–3½ hours

Terrain: Good grassy tracks at lower levels,
rougher or trackless on the highest land.

While driving south-west along the A595 trunk road from Broughton, or from across the Duddon Sands, the eye is drawn by the shadows and screes of Black Combe and hardly notices the adjacent but lower grass-topped rounded hill separated from its larger neighbour by a deep valley. White Combe's features are less dramatic but its ascent gives an interesting and straightforward walk which is well worth doing on a day of good visibility.

Although on the approach from Broughton you may see a sign on the roadside reading 'White Combe', I suggest you do not start from here, thus avoiding both parking difficulties and an uphill walk back later.

The best parking is on the side of the A595 at Beckside (grid ref 154847) opposite the end of the tree-lined lane leading up the valley of the Whitecombe Beck. A short walk along this soon passes the point where the metalled track turns across the beck to the converted Whicham Mill with its lovely garden. Keeping on the right (east) bank, a grass track now leads through two gates, after which it crosses by a footbridge to the left bank of the beck and continues up the valley beside it, below steep, bracken-covered fellsides. A stream joins the valley from the right, just beyond the rocks of Swine Crag, and a little spoil-tip marks the slit of an old copper-mine adit driving into the fellside underneath the track.

A little further along the track forks, just *before* the confluence with Blackcombe Beck is reached (this is not as the OS map indicates). The left-hand fork looks the better but it quickly fades at the confluence; the right-hand one leads to a ford over the beck and a path then zigzags upwards to use an obvious grassy rake slanting across the flank of White Combe. This leads almost to the top of the gill at Whitecombe Head but cuts back right just before getting there. If

White Combe, on the right, seen from the Whicham Valley

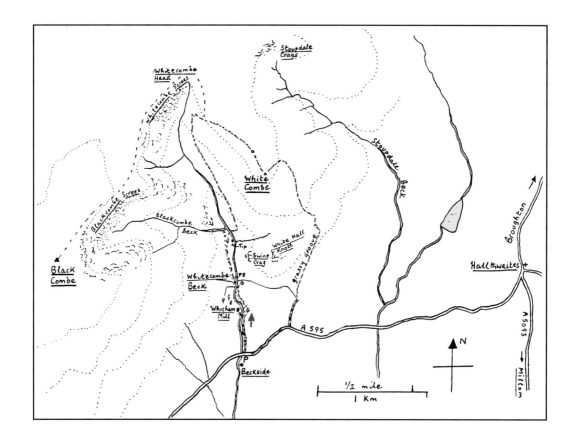

you turn back sharp left again at the end of this 'zag', you may follow a good path above Whitecombe Screes and southwards to Black Combe.

For White Combe, however, at the end of the 'zig' simply continue forwards to the south-east and make your way across the rolling prairie ahead, aiming for the obvious pile of stones seen at a slightly lower altitude. These harbour a circular stone shelter and provide a good spot to contemplate the view. To the south is Isle of Walney and Barrow; to the north-east is Coniston Old Man and its surrounding fells; Black-combe Screes are seen to the south-west and in the near distance, due north, is the little outcrop of Stoupdale Crags. There is little else, apart from a few sheep.

There is no obvious descent path from the shelter. Those shown on the maps hardly exist on the high land but an initial descent to the north-east, curving south-east, soon discloses the line of an old drove track slanting down a grassy groove to reach a gate at the end of an overgrown hedged lane. After a tussle with the vegetation, this leads to the main A595 and Beckside is a short distance along it to the right. Bearing in mind that this is a winding and busy main road with no footpath, there is something to be said for not entering the overgrown lane but turning right, beside and outside the intake wall. This contours round below Swine Crag and soon returns you to the valley of the Whitecombe Beck.

Whicham Mill

13. Tarn Hill and Stickle Pike from near Ulpha

Best Map: OS 1:25 000 Outdoor Leisure 6, South Western area

Distance: About 4½ miles/7.2km

Highest elevation reached: 1230ft/375m

Height gained: About 1125ft/343m

Star rating: **/***

Level of exertion: Medium

Time for the round: About 3 hours

Terrain: On sometimes rather vague grassy paths and open fell, so not suitable for misty weather.

This is a most interesting walk over the low but rugged Dunnerdale Fells, visiting no fewer than eight tarns on Tarn Hill (possibly the greatest concentration in the Lake District) and the splendid little summit of Stickle Pike en route.

The start is from the narrow, winding road leading north from the A595 at Duddon Bridge towards the little hamlet of Ulpha, at the southern end of the Duddon valley. Towards Ulpha, where the road runs close to the river, it is particularly beautiful, with woods and tumbling cataracts and you can park in a disused quarry just before a bend at the bottom of a rise in the road (grid ref 198920).

Don't start a futile search for the start of the right-of-way path shown on the OS map north of here but just go uphill to the east on a vague path through scattered yew trees, rowans and hollies behind the quarry. This soon crosses Cinderhill Beck (named from the old bloomeries or forges nearby) and a grassy way, which is clearly the line of the old path, then rises across fellside below a line of crags, heading south-east, towards a wide notch on the knobbly skyline ahead. A little further on, a little col is reached (at grid ref 212913), with a view down the other side to the secluded hamlet and green fields of Broughton Mills.

From the col, a definite path climbs steeply uphill to the north, quickly reaching the first objective, the trig point and cairn on Great Stickle. It is a good viewpoint, but one's eye soon travels along a line of knobbly tops to the sharply-pointed Stickle Pike, modest in height but as proud as any of the Lakeland giants. On the way over there, hiding in the folds of the land, are the many tarns of Tarn Hill, all eight being visible from the highest knobble. The only

Stickle Tarn, with Caw on the skyline

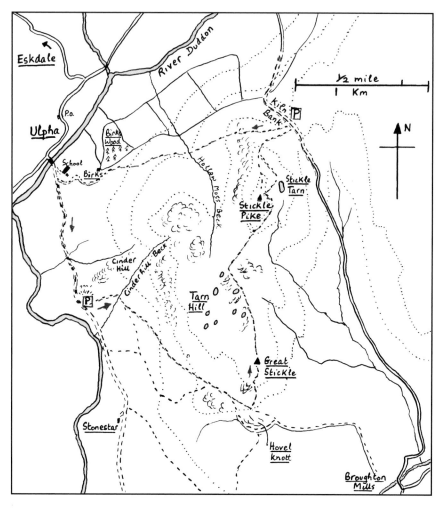

other place I can think of in Lakeland which has such a concentration of tarns is the top of Blake Rigg, the one above Blea Tarn in Little Langdale, but those are all tiny tarns. These are all bigger and on slightly different levels; two of them are almost full of reeds. Stickle Pike rises just beyond a depression. A direct attack on its steep and rocky front is likely to be repulsed, but a grassy path leads round to its east (right) side, and its double-topped summit, each with its own cairn, is quickly reached by an easy scramble. There are superb views, particularly north-east towards Caw.

Leaving the tops, a good path leads down the north side, passing the attractive Stickle Tarn just a little lower, and soon reaching a metalled road (from the Duddon valley to Broughton Mills) at its highest point, Kiln Bank Cross (grid ref 215933, where there is also a useful car park area). From here a path is shown on the OS map going almost due west and a faint grassy path does lead in that direction, gently climbing a little, then sneaking over a shoulder on Stickle Pike, but then it fades. Fortunately, the settlement at Ulpha soon comes into sight below and the line of the path is down brackeny fellside, with an intake wall on the right. Don't go through the gate in the wall but cross Hollow Moss Beck, aiming for the corner of Birks Wood and linking up a line of old mine-levels with their little spoil-tips, which leads down a natural rake to the house at Birks. The metalled drive now winds down to the road and a left turn soon leads back to the quarry.

14. Park Head Road and Long Mire Beck

Best Map: OS 1:25 000 Outdoor Leisure 6, South Western area

Distance: About 4 miles/6.4km

Highest elevation reached: About 1020ft/311m

Height gained: About 260ft/79m

Star rating: */* * *

Level of exertion: Low

Time for the round: About 2 hours

Terrain: On a good track, then grassy paths; can be a bit wet underfoot in the middle section.

Ignoring that the main valley of the River Duddon is sometimes named 'Dunnerdale', there is an adjacent, much smaller valley drained by the Dunnerdale Beck, flowing south to Broughton Mills. Half of the 'Dunnerdale skyline' (if such a grand title may be attributed to these minor but wonderfully knobbly fells) has already been covered in Walk 13 over Great Stickle and Stickle Pike. The other half of it is not a ridge at all but really a group of almost separate fells centring on the old Stainton Ground Quarries. An interesting walk can nevertheless be made around, rather than along, these; much better than it may appear on the map.

The walk has the distinct advantage of beginning at a height of 850ft/259m at the top of Kiln Bank, the hause where the minor road from the Duddon Valley leads to Broughton Mills (grid ref 215933); there is room for half a dozen cars here. (It is incidentally a good place for a miniscule walk up Stickle Pike if that is all you can manage.) Going east from the col, a level grassy track curves round a little hump with some slate spoil at its foot where the path passes above one old mine level and immediately below another before turning a corner to the left and descending slightly to join a substantial grassy track. Turn left along this, the Park Head Road, which links the true Dunnerdale with the other, the Duddon Valley. A short way along this a grassier but still clear way curves off to the right towards a great cave in the fellside, one of the former quarries of the old Stainton Ground. Do not take this, but stay on the 'road' initially contouring across open fell until a wall appears on the left. The highest point on the 'road' is reached shortly afterwards; it is in fact very little higher but it is a definite pass between a rocky bluff on the left and higher ground on the right and there is a

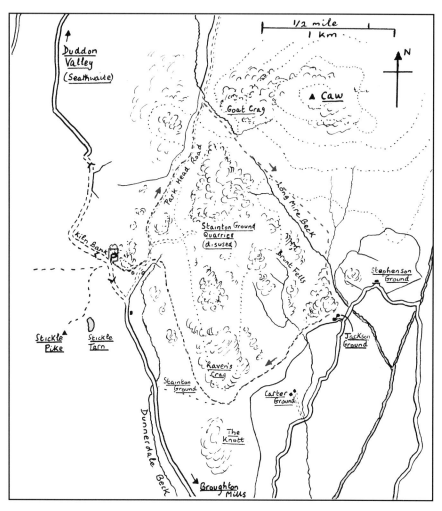

good view over the other side to the Duddon Valley. The splendid little mountain of Caw, the finest in this part of the Duddon Valley, is clearly in view from here.

Carry on downhill on the 'road' but only as far as a little stream crossing. Here turn back right (south-east) and a green path climbs to a new col, with the steep rocks of Goat Crag on the left. Now shadow the aptly named Long Mire Beck downhill on pleasant grass slopes between rock outcrops and at an easy angle, keeping to the north bank. The intake walls, green fields and buildings of the farm at Stephenson Ground come into view as you descend but, before reaching it, trend to the right (south) on a vague path crossing Long Mire Beck and then leading round the end of a rocky outcrop to find the buildings of the farm at Jackson Ground. These are hidden from sight until you are almost upon them although the farm dogs will probably advertise your presence with their barking.

Turn right here alongside the intake wall and a good green path now rises in a series of loops to a shoulder between The Knott and Raven's Crag. Here you turn north-west and follow a delightful green path contouring the fellside beyond and rising gently back to the mine-levels that you passed on the outward walk. You can probably see your car as well. I hope so; if you can't, it has either rolled away, been stolen or you are in the wrong place.

View to the Duddon Valley from beside the Park Head road

15. Caw and White Pike from Seathwaite

Best Map: OS 1:25 000 Outdoor Leisure 6, South
  Western area

Distance: About 6 miles/9.6km

Highest elevation reached: 1735ft/529m

Height gained: About 1400ft/427m (or about
  1100ft/335m, see text)

Star rating: * *

Level of exertion: Medium/high

Time for the round: About 4 hours

Terrain: Good paths, rough tracks, open fell paths
  or grass.

Caw is a shapely mountain of concave grassy and rocky slopes rising to a pointed top recognizable for miles, a worthy minor peak of the Duddon Valley. This walk gains height easily (if going uphill is ever easy) by using the Walna Scar Road, then sneaking in on Caw where its defences are lowest.

Parking may be found in Seathwaite opposite the little church (grid ref 229962), just north of the Newfield Inn, or at the unmetalled end of the Walna Scar Road (see sketch map). From the church, walk up the road beside Tarn Beck, then take a metalled track, signed for Turner Hall Farm. When this turns right towards the house, go straight ahead, and follow the path round and across level meadows to the north-east to an isolated house, High Moss; this is now an outdoor pursuits centre. Beyond this and to the left, a gate leads across a field to another; turn right on reaching the Walna Scar Road. The tarmac section ends at a gate, beyond which a track swings left for Seathwaite Tarn and the rougher path continues ahead (east). The other parking is through this gate.

A steady and perhaps tedious climb follows beside Long House Gill, with a forward prospect of open moorland. It is not very enticing, but some extensive old slate spoil-tips (the Walna Scar Quarries) become more noticeable below the skyline. Halfway up the moor, the path leaves the main gill and heads towards the spoil-tips and a gate in the wall below them. From here you have a choice of ways: stay on the path or go via the quarries; the latter route avoids the climb by traversing the fellside. The main path rises steeply beyond this gate, then slants away left up Walna Scar Side to reach the top of the ridge at the hause just below Brown Pike. If you go this way, now simply turn south along the ridge and a faint path bypasses the top of White Maiden to reach White Pike, from

The Dow Crag – Walna Scar ridge seen from the Duddon Valley

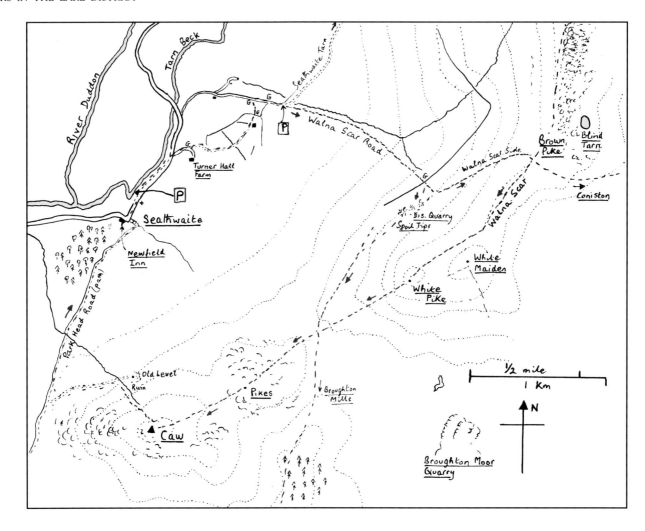

where you look down on the Broughton Moor Slate Quarry.

There is an exhilarating descent from White Pike, south-west towards Caw, down tongues of grass between rock buttresses to scree and easier slopes, passing a little stone ruin (not on the OS map), to reach a broad col. Here you join a green path traversing from the Walna Scar Quarries, the one you could have used instead of going over White Pike. The grassy path from the col towards Broughton Mills is very little used, which is not surprising as it is exceptionally boggy and also leads away from Caw, so you need to leave it and rise over rough grassy slopes to the west to reach a subsidiary height with a few rock spikes and a cairn. This is spot height 469, Pikes. A short descent on the other side leads to the last ascent of the walk, up steepening and rockier slopes, to reach the trig point on Caw where there are various intriguing initials and dates marked on the summit rock. From here you may see quite clearly to the hamlet of Seathwaite with its little church almost hidden amongst trees.

A tiny stream rises high on the north-west slopes of Caw and its start is soon reached by descending in that direction and then following its course downhill on the easy grass slopes beside it. When an abandoned mine level and tip, together with a roofless building, are reached, an embanked grassy track begins which slants downhill at an easy angle to join the old track of the Park Head Road at a gate in a wall corner. A right turn down this track, overlooking the delightful

The descent to Seathwaite down the Park Head road

Duddon Valley landscape and by-passing a very fine wood of oak and silver birch, soon leads back to Seathwaite just a few paces from the hospitality of the Newfield Inn.

16. Tarn Beck and Fickle Steps

Best Map: OS 1:25 000 Outdoor Leisure 6, South Western area

Distance: About 4 miles/6.4km

Highest elevation reached: About 700ft/213m

Height gained: About 650ft/198m

Star rating: * *

Level of exertion: Medium

Time for the round: About 3 hours

Terrain: Tremendous variety, from grassy paths to rough walking where you might not expect it.

This walk winds through woods, across open pastures, beside chattering becks and over or around some of the many fine rock outcrops that make the Duddon Valley landscape so enchanting. The crossing of the Fickle Steps is a little adventure.

Start from the Forestry Commission's Froth Pot car park beside the River Duddon (grid ref 235996), three miles north of Seathwaite. From here, walk about 200 paces north-east, up the valley ignoring a footpath sign on the right, and continue just beyond this to a broad forestry track on the right. Go along this until you round a bend, then turn back sharp right along an obvious track. This dwindles to a path, then almost fizzles out as it rises through the plantation, reaching a partly collapsed wall near the top of a rise. Continue in the same direction (south-east) and follow this old wall beneath the dark trees over a rise and downhill to where a little beck drains into a boggy, sloping field, The Close. A stile here confirms that you are on route, but does not give much help as to where the path goes now. However, climb to the south-east, up the left side of The Close, and the boggy land is quickly left behind as you reach a dry grassy path now shadowing the main intake wall. Turn right here and follow this path southwards, passing a gateway in the wall and then slanting down to another gateway and ladder-stile seen just ahead. The faint path continues down the valley until you meet the lively Tarn Beck just below some waterfalls. Although the path officially crosses the beck, other walkers have avoided a possible wetting by keeping to the right (west) bank. It is fairly rough ground on either side but a footbridge comes into view ahead (grid ref 236977, not shown on the OS map) which you can use or not as necessary so long as you find yourself on the west bank when you reach the next one, which is opposite Tongue House.

The footbridge across Tarn Beck

63

Looking towards Troutal from The Close

A better path now leads to the house and barn of Thrang, passes behind them and along an old track beneath trees. This trends away from the fields, rising to the north-west round the southern tip of the rocky and wooded High Tongue. Skirting a boggy bit of land the unfenced metalled road is gained, just opposite a public bridleway sign (and where a few cars may be parked). The path down the far slope leads to the Fickle Steps, a line of stepping stones across the River Duddon. The crossing is protected by a wire cable; but it is rather slack, so that if you feel yourself seeming to teeter to one side, it will let you do so before its restraining influence is thankfully felt. This will, of course, occur in mid-stream as you reach the widest gap at the deepest place. But I don't think anybody has drowned here. So far.

After this little excitement, turn right on the path alongside the river. The Forestry Commission sign says the path is 'rough and bouldery in places' and it does not exaggerate as it dodges through the trees and over roots and along sections of duck-boarding which still manage to leave some of the quagmire unbridged; look upon it as an obstacle course and you will enjoy it. Having passed Troutal Farm, just glimpsed on the far bank, the path rises away from the river towards Birks but a signed permissive path to Birks Bridge soon leads to more open woodland, declining gently to this famous little packhorse bridge. Cross it, turn left and the car park is just up the road.

Crossing the Fickle Steps

17. Seathwaite Tarn from the Duddon Valley

Best Map: OS 1:25 000 Outdoor Leisure 6, South
    Western area

Distance: About 4 miles/6.4km (add 2 miles/3.2km
    if you circle the tarn)

Highest elevation reached: About 1250ft/381m

Height gained: About 780ft/238m

Star rating: **

Level of exertion: Medium

Time for the round: About 2½ hours (add 1 hour if
    you circle the tarn)

Terrain: On grassy paths, not always obvious and
    sometimes rough.

Seathwaite Tarn hides in a high and rocky combe above the Duddon Valley and this walk to it passes through some most delightful landscape.

There is parking for a few cars in a little layby (grid ref 231975) about 1 mile/1.6km north of Seathwaite where the road is unfenced after crossing Seathwaite Bridge and is itself crossed by a public footpath. From the parking place a public footpath sign can be seen pointing south-east down the right-hand side of a boggy field but it is better to descend on the left side, as you look downhill, when a dry, grassy path materializes. This curves round the tip of High Tongue, one of the fine little eminences that make the Duddon Valley so attractive, then enters a narrow belt of trees. Ignore stiles on the right and follow the path behind a barn and then behind the house and barn of Thrang. Fifty paces further on the path forks, with the right hand one leading towards Tarn Beck and which will be joined on the return; the left-hand one now rises to the north, through trees and between rocks, quickly becoming a grassy path through bracken on the slopes of High Tongue and leading to a stile over a transverse wall. From here this path wanders over and around a series of hummocks and boggy places on Troutal Tongue, with fine views up the valley and to Harter Fell, then descends to the road, reaching it at the point where it becomes walled at a cattle-grid.

Veering right here (footpath sign), the path leads alongside a wall to Brow Side Farm, rising beyond it to a gate. A little further on, as the path becomes vague in a boggy area, turn up the slope on the right towards the substantial intake wall traversing the fellside higher up. A gateway in this, partly hidden from below by a rock outcrop, leads to an obvious path climbing a steep but short slope beyond, the

Looking north up the Duddon Valley from above The Close

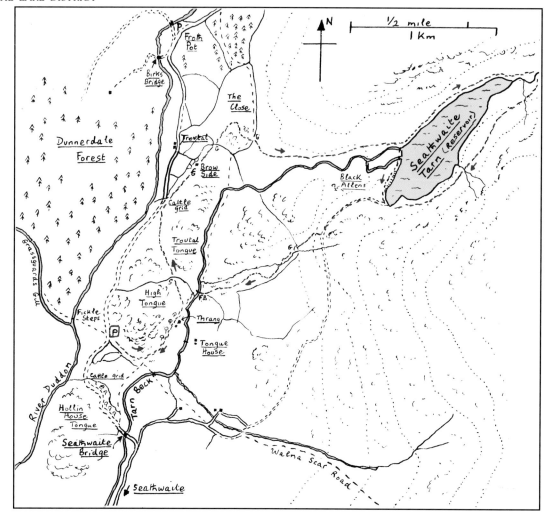

angle soon easing. Before long the thin line of what can only be the top of the dam holding Seathwaite Tarn comes into view and the path skirts below craggy fellside over undulating ground to reach it.

A little-used path leads round the tarn, keeping fairly close to the water's edge on the west side, where it passes a little rock island looking like the grey hump of a great whale, then leads further into the deep combe before crossing the feeder stream and returning. On the south-east shore, steep crags fall into the water and so the path takes a higher line to avoid them. On a fine day, it is a grand circuit; on a day of low cloud it will seem less attractive and is then best avoided by crossing the dam wall, to join the gravel track at the south-west end of the dam. Follow this. Below the dam wall is an area of boulders surrounded by bog, named Black Allens, which I found of particular interest because my father told me when I was a lad that the Allens had come out of a bog somewhere, although I thought he said it was in Ireland.

Follow the track until it swings south, then turn off it down a grassy path leading south-west. Passing a sheepfold at a gate, follow the course of a little beck downhill, then down a grassy groove to a gate and ladder-stile near the valley bottom. Leading forward across a boggy area, a second ladder-stile is reached and immediately beyond it is a footbridge over Tarn Beck. Turn left on the far side and you are back at the house and barn of Thrang and can reverse the last bit of the start of the route back to the car.

Looking north from near Troutal Tongue

18. Harter Fell from Froth Pot

Best Map: OS 1:25 000 Outdoor Leisure, South
  Western area

Distance: About 4¼ miles/6.8km

Highest elevation reached: 2142ft/653m

Height gained: About 1550ft/473m

Star rating: **

Level of exertion: Medium/high

Time for the round: About 3 hours

Terrain: Good paths, good (and bad) Forestry
  tracks and open fell walking on grass.

This way of climbing one of the finest of the lower fells, the rugged Harter Fell, is one of the walks in this book which, as promised in the introduction, is short but not necessarily easy, not only because of the steepness of the uphill climb but because it is perfectly obvious that the Forestry Commission have not done much for years to maintain the right-of-way paths shown on the OS maps; in some cases, they have virtually disappeared. The walk is still a good one despite this.

The Forestry Commission's car park at Froth Pot (grid ref 235996) beside the River Duddon, 4 miles/6.4km south from the Wrynose Pass or 3 miles/4.8 km north from Seathwaite, is the starting point. About 200 paces south down the road, the River Duddon thunders through a deep gorge, spanned by Birks Bridge. Cross the bridge, and the track on its far side immediately makes a loop round to the south and rises through glades of oak and silver birch in Great Wood to reach a short walled lane and grassy track leading to Birks; this was formerly a farm but is currently a field study centre. The track from this leads to a gate, then curves rightwards to merge with a broad Forestry track (leading back to Froth Pot). There has been much felling of timber in this area which confuses the route-finding, so turn sharp left here along this main track, but only for fifty paces. The path now goes off to the right, uphill over rough and rather rutted ground, with some sheep-folds on the right, a wall on the left and the clean grey rock of Buck Crag peeping above the conifers on the right. Walk up open ground on the edge of the forest for about 200 paces and then turn right again, west, off this path and up a rather boggy break in the timber. Here, if it survives, you *may* find a post marked 'Harter Fell 2140ft not waymarked beyond here' which will not worry you since any waymarks so far have been invisible.

Press on beside (or sometimes in) a little stream up

The south-east face of Harter Fell from near Seathwaite Tarn

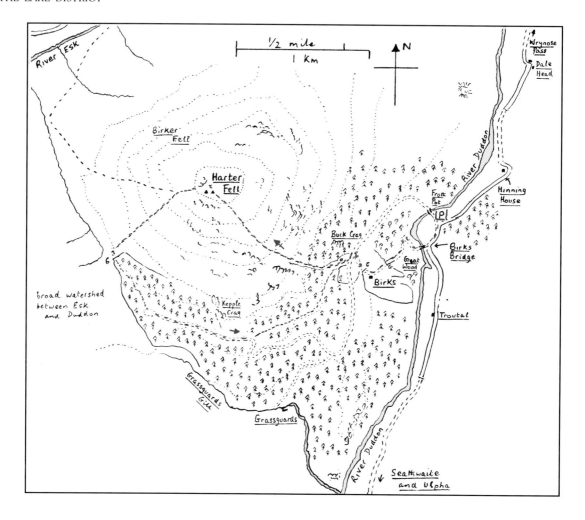

this narrowing break through dense and fragrant forest, anxiously consulting your compass from time to time to stay on 285 degrees magnetic, until the trees thin, you find yourself in a wide gully and, looking back downhill over the jungle, you can see Birks again. The way now becomes much clearer, rising steadily up an open, easy but steep gully, with an occasional cairn to mark the route, and leading to open grass slopes traversed by a wire fence and stile. Beyond this, the faint path winds up between outcrops to cross a little depression and reach the final rocky pyramid of Harter Fell, with its trig point and triple summits. It's a splendid viewpoint.

Leaving the top, an obvious cairned path leads off to the west and should be followed for a short way, but not too far or you may find yourself actually in Eskdale; look for a fainter path which turns off to the south-west, heads for the broad watershed between the Rivers Esk and Duddon, and reaches the northwestern tip of the forest. A gate and path now lead back into the timber, battling over tree roots, but soon reaches a good Forestry track at a turning circle. Don't waste time looking for a footpath on the right of this track for it has been smothered by the timber; stay on the track until it takes a sharp right turn downhill (grid ref 222987) and here go straight ahead (northeast) on a path heading through a break in the forest. This soon starts to descend quite steeply and you find yourself at the sheepfold and Forestry track outside Birks, from where the outward route is reversed back to the start.

Birks Bridge

73

19. Buck Barrow to Devoke Water: A Traverse

Best Map: OS 1:25 000 Outdoor Leisure 6, South
Western area but note that the start is not on
this map. With this in mind, the best map is
OS 1:50 000 Landranger 96 Barrow-in-Furness

Distance: About 6½ miles/10.4km

Highest elevation reached: 1880ft/573m

Height gained: About 1000ft/305m

Star rating: * *

Level of exertion: Medium

Time for the traverse: About 3 hours

Terrain: Fairly high open fell, mostly grass with
just vague paths, but straightforward in clear
conditions.

This is the only traverse in this book, but I consider it justifiable on the grounds of its quality, linking the points of high land north of Black Combe along the western seaboard of the Lake District. It is easy enough for a willing partner to drop you off at the start and collect you three hours later at the end of the bridleway leading to Devoke Water (grid ref 171976);

then you can drive to the fleshpots of Ravenglass and visit Muncaster Castle as a thank-you.

Start at the highest point of the very scenic fell road (with views all the way to the Scafells) that links Broughton in Furness with Waberthwaite (grid ref 149897), where four or five cars can also be conveniently parked. The first of the high points on the traverse, Buck Barrow, is in view from here, the right-hand of three groups of rocks on the higher land to the north. A wall leads up towards the rocks, with a grassy track alongside it, but it climbs towards the middle of the three rock groups (the left-hand one is Kinmont Buckbarrow, made less accessible by a new wire fence), so trend away from the wall to reach the little sharp-pointed cairn on Buck Barrow itself, which is also the highest of the rock groups; from here, enjoy views to the sea and to Black Combe in the south. Then an easy descent through the rocks on Buck Barrow's top leads to a fairly boggy depression drained by Logan Beck. The most boring bit of the walk now follows, a tramp across grassy slopes slanting up to Whitfell, with a few boulders amongst the grass to relieve the monotony. Fortunately there is a clear objective, the very substantial cairn on the summit near to a little windbreak and which is definitely higher than the nearby trig-point.

*Looking south-west from
Buck Barrow to the
Duddon Sands*

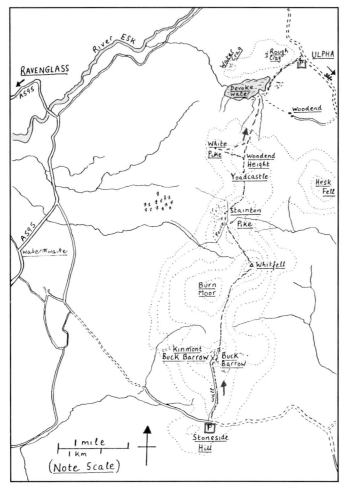

Stainton Pike, to the north again, is lower than Whitfell and so, apart from the last little rise beyond a depression, the walk across to it is a descent. In the depression is the small and shallow Holehouse Tarn, in a magnificent position, with views beyond it as far as Pillar above Ennerdale. To touch the summit cairn on the Pike you will need to step over a low wire fence but while there you may peer down the rough fell to the north-west, roughly towards Ravenglass: here there was a Roman port and you can fancy you can glimpse traces of the ancient British 'city of Barnscar' showing through the earth that now buries it. Recross the fence and head north-east towards the broad-based round-topped rocky pile of Yoadcastle, seen further north again. Grassy rakes give an easy scramble to its top and a view to Devoke Water, which you know must now be hiding in the vast depression beyond, might justifiably be expected. Not yet. The cairnless Yoadcastle must be left and the cairned top of Woodend Height, just a little further, must be reached before Devoke Water does come into sight, looking a surprisingly long way below, with views to Eskdale beyond. A short walk to the west gives a diversion to White Pike, its little summit crowned by a tall and very slender cairn.

From here, a grassy descent through little rock outcrops and, with just the odd sheep track, leads down towards the water's edge. Here you will pick up the path and then the firm track which quickly leads to the fell road between Ulpha and Eskdale Green, where your transport is, I hope, waiting.

20. A Circuit of Devoke Water

<table>
<tr><td>

Best Map: OS 1:25 000 Outdoor Leisure 6, South Western area

Distance: About 4¾ miles/7.6km

Highest elevation reached: 1621ft/494m

Height gained: About 740ft/226m

Star rating: */* *

Time for the round: About 2½ hours

Terrain: Largely on open fell with faint paths; boggy at the west end of Devoke Water.

</td></tr>
</table>

Devoke Water lies in a depression on a broad shelf above Eskdale and is presumably occasionally visited by angling parties, for there is a two-storied boathouse on the shore. I believe that this, the largest tarn in Lakeland, was originally stocked with trout brought from Italy (although I have my doubts about that) by the monks of Furness Abbey centuries ago. The luxuriant heather which clothes the surrounding ring of low fells encourages a feeling of being in the Scottish Highlands and I'm sure many a dram has been swallowed here by fishermen in the past. These same low fells provide splendid vantage points for many greater ones, particularly those at the head of Eskdale and Wasdale which can be clearly seen on a good day. This walk is a circuit of these low fells and its chief aim is the enjoyment of the long-range views, so avoid misty weather.

The unenclosed fell road between Ulpha and Eskdale offers many superb views but none better than where it comes round a bend and starts the descent to Eskdale, marked as a viewpoint by the OS. Just beyond this, a finger-post marks a junction where a track is signed right to Stanley Gill and one goes left (although the signed bit is, at the time of writing, missing) to Devoke Water (grid ref 171976). A couple of cars can park here.

Take the track as far as a gate-post and then turn off, just north of west, up a heather slope, with Devoke Water coming into view below, to reach the boulder-topped Rough Crag, the first of the ring of hills. Here there is a cairn and, next to it, a circular copper knob about 2 inches in diameter and looking rather like the top of a mushroom; there is no triangulation column but this knob is perhaps something to do with the OS. There is a wonderful view to Boot in Eskdale, to Great Gable and Kirk Fell, to Slight Side and Scafell.

Water Crag is obviously the next high point to visit, although its top is largely grass; the 'crag' is down the slope to the north. From here, descend

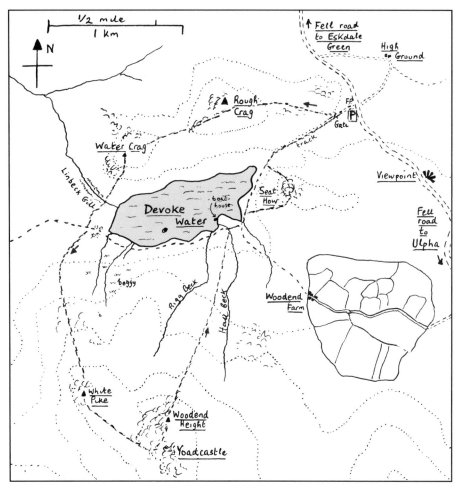

towards the western outflow of Devoke Water, crossing it just before it enters the rocky groove of Linbeck Gill; then pass what the OS map marks as ancient cairns but which look more like hollowed-out windbreaks. A tall rock column, a carefully constructed cairn on White Pike, can be seen on the skyline up the slope to the south and this, after traversing some boggy ground requiring delicate choice of the firmest bits, is the next objective. A steady ascent, good for the constitution, soon leads to it with views out to sea, to the full length of Muncaster Fell and Muncaster Castle.

To the south-east now are the two remaining high points on the circuit, and an easier-angled ascent next leads to the broad-based round-topped rocky pyramid of Yoadcastle. Surprisingly, for this is clearly the higher of the two, there is no cairn here and you must continue the extra two hundred paces or so to find one on Woodend Height which is, in itself, a much less distinguished top. It is, however, a much better viewpoint, the finest on the circuit and well worth the effort needed to reach it.

The descent to the north-east, making for the boathouse on the side of Devoke Water, where the track back to the car is met, is straightforward, although a short diversion to scramble up the last little rocky height of Seat How will appeal to youngsters of all ages before following the dirt track back to the parking place.

Devoke Water from Woodend Height

21.   Blea Tarn, Siney Tarn and the River Esk

Best Map: OS 1:25 000 Outdoor Leisure 6, South
Western area

Distance: About 4½ miles/7.2km

Highest elevation reached: 951ft/290m

Height gained: About 800ft/244m

Star rating: * * *

Level of exertion: Medium

Time for the round: About 2½ hours

Terrain: Mostly on good grass or firm tracks;
occasionally boggy.

This short and comparatively low-level walk in beautiful Eskdale is a delight at any season. The little climb to Blea Tarn gives some good exercise and the walk as a whole is memorable for the variety of its landscape, even on a day of poor weather.

The best car park is that beside Dalegarth Station at the Eskdale terminus of the Ravenglass to Eskdale miniature railway (grid ref 174007). From here, walk south-west down the road to cross the Whillan Beck and, on the other side of the bridge, cross the railway line running alongside the road to a gate with a finger-post sign 'Blea Tarn'. A grassy path, occasionally on an old embankment, now winds pleasantly up brackeny fellside to the north, curving leftwards as height is gained and giving some grand views both up and down Eskdale as it does. At one point it looks as though a choice of ways has to be made but both paths quickly climb to the broad ridge above. Blea Tarn is soon found in a little hollow edged with ice-smoothed craglets on its Eskdale side. Bleatarn Hill is only a short distance north-east of the tarn and will obviously provide a comprehensive view of the terrain ahead, so it is well worth climbing to its rocky little top, soon reached by diverting from a path that passes close by the summit cairn. Apart from a splendid all-round view, the glint of water can be seen from here on Siney Tarn, the next objective, while beyond and to the left of a dark line of conifers climbing out of Miterdale is an interesting ridge of grassy hollows and rocky outcrops, which is where the walk now heads.

Returning to the south end of Blea Tarn, the path leads north-west past Siney Tarn which is almost split into several distinct pools by invading rushes, and then becomes indistinct on boggy land. A solitary rowan is a good point at which to change direction to the west-south-west, and a better path soon winds

Looking up Eskdale from the path up to Blea Tarn

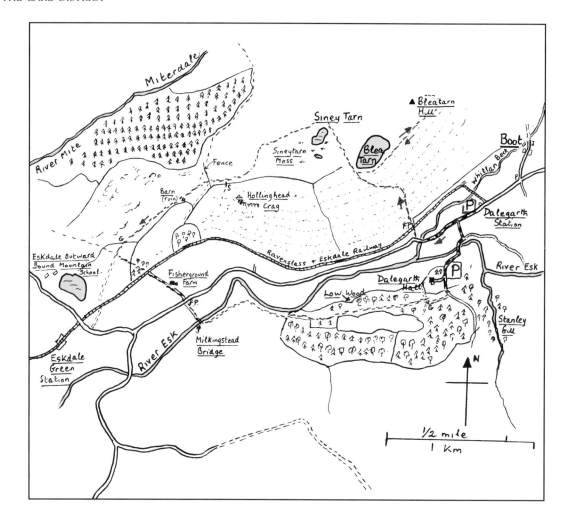

round Sineytarn Moss on its drier edge until it is alongside a wall. Ignore the ladder-stile over this and continue beside the wall down a little slope to a gate in a wire fence, then take the higher of two paths beyond to reach a roofless barn. From here, a delightful grassy path slants across the fellside below smoothed granite crags and then passes through a gateway in a transverse wall. Continue for only a hundred yards or so, then turn sharp left (south-east) alongside a fence, through a gap in a wall and then through woodland to reach and cross the railway again. The walled lane now leads past Fisherground Farm (a popular place for camping, caravans and chalets) to the road. Here a finger-post directly opposite points the way across the field to Milking-stead Bridge, its footway supported on steel cables, and you should now turn left.

The last stage is initially marked by bridleway signs, rambling through birch and rowan woodland near the waterside, then, as the river swings away, it passes through Low Wood, notable for some giant oaks and particularly tall conifers. Stay on the main track until it reaches a T-junction with another, directly in front of a wall beyond which can be seen the five tall chimneys of Dalegarth Hall. Turn right here and follow the track through a gate, across a field and back onto another track, circling the Hall. You shortly pass Trough House Bridge car park, on the right, then follow the metalled road beyond it round to the main Eskdale road again. Dalegarth Station is just up the road to the right.

Old barn on the descent towards Eskdale Green

22. The Stone Circles and Boat How from Boot

Best Map: OS 1:25 000 Outdoor Leisure 6, South Western area

Distance: About 5 miles/8km

Highest elevation reached: 1106ft/337m

Height gained: About 950ft/290m

Star rating: **

Level of exertion: Low/medium

Time for the round: About 2½ hours

Terrain: On good tracks and grassy paths, although the latter are rather vague on the higher land. Avoid a day of poor visibility.

High on the broad grassy fell north of Boot in Eskdale are a number of ancient stone circles, as puzzling and inscrutable as always. This walk visits them, then continues to Burnmoor Tarn for some superb views.

Start from the large car park next to Dalegarth Station, terminus of the Ravenglass to Eskdale miniature railway (grid ref 174007). Walk north-west from here up the road, past Brook House and left into the attractive little village of Boot. Cross the little hump-backed bridge over the Whillan Beck, past the restored cornmill (as the tarmac ends) and enter an alternately grassy and stony track, between walls, which rises to the north. Ignore the gate on the right leading to a track at a lower level, which will be used on the return, and continue up the walled lane. You will shortly have a good sight of Slight Side, the ridge rising to Scafell, over the wall on the right. The lane soon ends at a group of six byres or barns, five of which are quite derelict, and the track leads out onto open grassy fell. It continues to the north, becoming less clear as it does, but turns west where there are two obvious boulders on the left and then a distinctive little rock outcrop sticking up out of the moor ahead. Go up onto this and two of the stone circles will be immediately seen nearby.

As is so often the case, these are out on a wide moor, surrounded by higher mountains and within sight of the sea. The largest has about forty stones, only a few of which still stand, in a circle of about thirty-five paces in diameter. Unusually, there are four or perhaps five smaller inner circles with central pits. A smaller main circle about a hundred paces to the north has eleven stones, all standing, again with an inner ring, while fifty paces to the south-west is

Scafell seen from the path to Boat How north of Boot

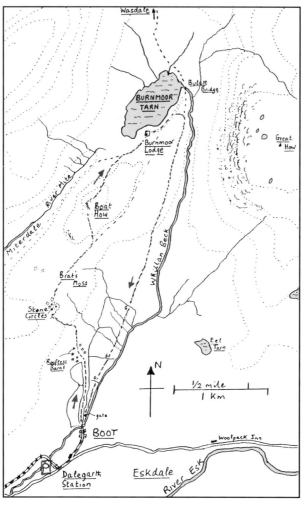

a third, again with eleven stones and also about eighteen paces in diameter.

From the two smaller circles a faint path leads NNE towards the higher land but soon starts to veer below it, so leave it – noticing another enigmatic circular pit of stones beside the path, only three paces in diameter and two feet deep. At first I took this to have been built to trap foxes, but it would have to be a dead fox to be unable to escape from this one. Easy slopes beyond lead to the little rock castle on Boat How. From its top, you have a first sight of Burnmoor Tarn, with a backdrop of the great Wasdale fells; by trending towards it and a little north you will soon pick up a path leading round to Burnmoor Lodge, in its own enclosure just above the shore. The building is shuttered, the tops of the chimneys slated over to keep weather (and jackdaws) out and there is a little box on one wall with a message on it reading 'A word for you, take one', suggesting that it was a repository for religious tracts. This thought is confirmed when you notice, high on the east wall, a plaque with a quotation from the Acts of the Apostles and eight lines of a hymn. It is certainly a fine, if very lonely, situation in which to contemplate the infinite.

An obvious grass track now curves from the Lodge towards the point where the outflow of the Whillan Beck from the tarn is crossed at Bulatt Bridge, but there is no necessity to go that far. Just curve over the toe of the moor to the south-east and you will quickly link up with the main grassy bridleway leading easily and pleasantly back to Boot and the start.

23. Eel Tarn and Stony Tarn from the Woolpack Inn

Best Map: OS 1:25 000 Outdoor Leisure 6, South
   Western area

Distance: About 4½ miles/7.2km

Highest elevation reached: 1302ft/397m

Height gained: About 1000ft/305m

Star rating: ***

Level of exertion: Medium

Time for the round: About 3 hours

Terrain: On good paths generally although not
   very clear in places on the higher open fell;
   some boggy bits.

The broad and hummocky ridge north-east of Boot in Eskdale gives excellent walking in a rugged and knobbly landscape full of visual delight; this particular walk links the two main tarns to give a most attractive round.

Start from the hospitable Woolpack Inn in Eskdale (grid ref 190010), where bar meals and other comforts are available, then turn up the lane left of the Inn yard (as seen from the front) between the buildings, rising to the north-east through an enclosed area.

Leaving this at a gate, a green path leads across a few boggy bits, with a wall on the left hand until it turns away downhill. This green path continues winding uphill, shortly passing a roofless barn, and then swings north while still climbing, until the angle eases and Eel Tarn comes into view to the right of the path. Like Langhow Tarn (also known as Youdell Tarn) found on the broad saddle between Easedale and Great Langdale, this one is colonised by raucous black-headed gulls.

Cross the small outflow on a stone slab at the northern end of the tarn, skirting round the marshy area, and pick up a made green track again, its edge buttressed by stones for a short distance. Beyond a grassy groove, the path fades but, keeping a north-easterly direction with higher ground on the right, Stony Tarn soon comes into view in a wide depression. The path then reappears ahead, skirting the left bank, and by-passing a circular sheep-fold near the shore; the easiest way is simply to follow it round.

Much more interesting, however, is to veer right towards the higher ground before descending towards the tarn to where a solitary square boulder is perched like a marker on top of a small group of rocks. According to the OS map this area has the delightful name of Peelplace Noddle, although precisely to what that name refers is not clear. Apart from the boulders,

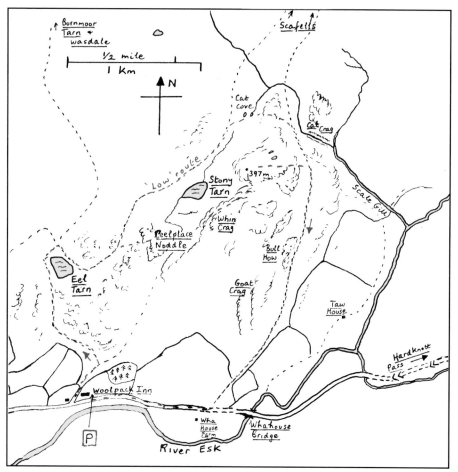

the heather and the innumerable little sheep tracks through it (there is not much grass for them up here), the object that now catches the eye, still on the high land above the tarn, is a cairn on a small but shapely peak directly ahead. This is Whin Crag and traces of path will be found leading to it, set in a commanding position high above Stony Tarn. From Whin Crag, a line of little rocky heights form a ridge to the north-east which then curves round the head of the tarn to another cairned height, marked as 397m on the OS map, an excellent viewpoint for the Scafell slopes but also for Bowfell and Crinkle Crags across Eskdale.

If you chose the 'low' route beside Stony Tarn, simply follow the path north-east in the direction of the Scafells, but leave it to turn east when just beyond the boggy area of Cat Cove and the main and well-used Scafell path via Slight Side is soon reached. From point 397m, this main Scafell path is not visible but by heading east down grassy rakes it will soon be spotted and is joined. This quickly reaches an edge beyond which a steeper path leads down Scale Gill but the main path takes an easier angle, down a linked line of broad rocky ledges which give a delightful descent, almost all on grass and with good views across Eskdale to the ruins of the Roman fort of Hard Knott. The road down Eskdale is joined opposite Wha House Farm and a ten-minute walk along it returns you to the Woolpack Inn.

View to the Scafells from near the head of Catcove Beck

24. Green Crag and Low Birker Tarn

Best Map: OS 1:25 000 Outdoor Leisure 6, South
  Western area

Distance: About 5¼ miles/8.4km

Highest elevation reached: 1604ft/489m

Height gained: About 1350ft/411m

Star rating: * * *

Level of exertion: Medium

Time for the round: About 3 hours

Terrain: Good grassy paths, vague paths on rough
  fell and a choice of either 'rock and heather' or
  'bog and grass' on the approach to Green
  Crag.

This is a short 'walk on the wild side' for walkers who appreciate making their way over sometimes vague paths on often rough and knobbly terrain.

You may park on the roadside just opposite Wha House Farm in Eskdale (grid ref 204008), or, if you patronise the friendly Woolpack Inn, you could start there. In either case, walk eastwards along the road and cross Whahouse Bridge. A grassy path now heads south across pasture to a footbridge, then swings left through a small wood to reach a gate, beyond which an obvious track continues into another small wood. At the far side of this, just outside the intake wall, is a finger-post with signs for both Hardknott and Penny Hill Farm. Turn left here for Hardknott but almost immediately fork right up Spothow Gill, passing a little spoil-tip beside the beck. This path climbs steeply up the wooded ravine but fades as height is gained. Cross the beck as the trees thin out, continuing to a stile over a wire fence beside a wall. On the other side is the well-used path rising to Harter Fell from the foot of Hardknott Pass, which is now joined.

The distinctive rounded and rocky top of Green Crag, the next main objective and the highest of the line of rocky summits continuing to the south from here, is not visible until you have continued a little further uphill. One branch of the main path soon forks left to climb Harter Fell; the other goes forward over the watershed but soon enters the forest. Rather than losing sight of your objective, step over the fence and swing in an arc south-west then west over grassy but rather boggy ground towards Green Crag. Alternatively, over much rougher but more interesting terrain, head for the nearest higher land, Dow Crag, to the south-west (from where you will have a distant view of Devoke Water), and then choose your

Green Crag, in the right distance, seen across Eskdale

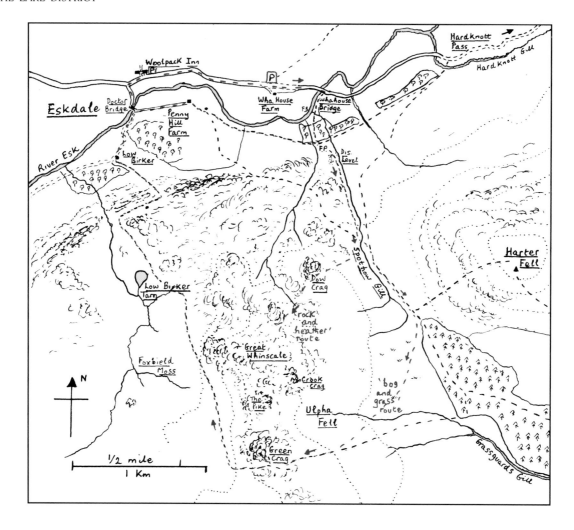

own line over the heathery, bouldery country that links the various high points (Great Whinscale, Crook Crag, The Pike) along the way to Green Crag.

Green Crag is an upthrust of compact slabs of rock seamed with fine cracks and grassy ledges, looking remarkably like Pike o'Stickle in Langdale when seen from its west side. From the cairn on its top you can see to Black Combe, to Whitfell, to Stickle Pike (Duddon) and to many other fells that you know are familiar but whose profile from here is subtly different.

The path shown on the OS map heading north from Green Crag towards Low Birker Tarn will need the eye of faith to locate on the ground as you descend towards the boggy depression of Foxbield Moss, but becomes obvious on the approach to the tarn. A good path leads down the depression beyond; then, on the lip of Eskdale once more, a delightful grassy path swings north-east, contours high above the valley below, passes a roofless barn, then descends in grassy zigzags through junipers to reach Low Birker, once a farm and now a guest-house. The track beyond soon leads to the River Esk at Doctor Bridge.

If you parked at the Woolpack Inn, you should cross the bridge and will be there in minutes. If you parked nearer to Whahouse Bridge, you may choose to walk along the road (perhaps with a diversion to the pub en route) or take the gravel track to Penny Hill Farm and the bridleway beyond it to link up with the outward route.

The approach across Foxbield Moss to Low Birker Tarn

25. Yewbarrow from Overbeck Bridge

Best Map: OS 1:25 000 Outdoor Leisure 6, South
    Western area

Distance: About 4 miles/6.4km

Highest elevation reached: 2060ft/628m

Height gained: About 1965ft/599m

Star rating: * * *

Level of exertion: Medium/high

Time for the round: About 3 hours

Terrain: A mixture of grassy paths, a stony gully
    and a rocky descent requiring particular care
    for a short distance.

Wasdale is home to Lakeland's deepest lake, Wastwater; to England's highest mountain, Scafell Pike, and is also accepted as the home of English rock-climbing. It is therefore appropriate that at least one of the walks in this collection should be here at the head of Wasdale and the rocky spine of Yewbarrow, overlooking Wastwater, gives a splendid short round with excellent views. It is also appropriate that a useful (if often denied) technique used in rock-climbing, namely the ability to descend ele-

gantly by using the friction of one's bottom, can be conveniently practised by walkers as well as climbers. Fortunately for the preservation of one's person and trousers it is only over a very short distance.

A good car park (voluntary fee) will be found at Overbeck Bridge just before reaching the head of Wastwater (grid ref 168068) and just at the foot of the south-west ridge of Yewbarrow. A path leads directly out of the car park to a kissing-gate, then turns to rise beside a wall and directly up the spine of the fell. There is a good view up Brown Tongue and into Hollow Stones below Scafell Pike although the great cliffs of Scafell are only seen in profile from here. The steeper rocks of Bell Rib soon rear up ahead and, continuing further, will lead to a worthwhile ascent up the nose for competent scramblers; walkers will cross the wall here by a ladder-stile and follow the path slanting across the fellside towards the ribs and buttresses of Dropping Crag. When the path forks, veer right and up a scree-filled gully between Dropping Crag and the higher rocks on Bell Rib to the right. It is a little more awkward where the gully narrows but then an easier angled groove curves rightwards to reach the Great Door, a notch in the crest of the rocky ridge from where, for an exhilarating moment, there is a dramatic view down a deep gully on the far side to Wastwater and over to Scafell

Yewbarrow seen from the road beside Wastwater

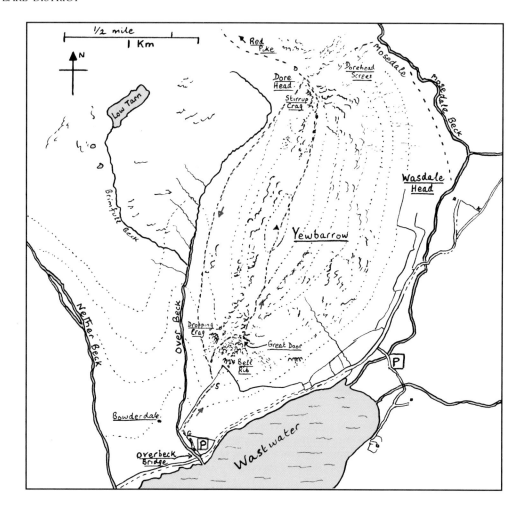

Pike. To the west, the best view is to Seatallan.

The ridge now gives delightful walking over grass and rocky outcrops to reach a cairn on the highest point of Yewbarrow and about half way along its length; then there is a depression followed by more undulations of the ridge, with the view ahead increasingly dominated by Red Pike and the steep slopes of Pillar and Kirk Fell rising above Mosedale. Two cairns, the first built on a stone slab, are passed, then quite suddenly the ridge comes to an abrupt end at the blunt nose of Stirrup Crag, with a dramatic drop virtually all the way from the ridge-top to the floor of Mosedale.

An obvious rock staircase leads down Stirrup Crag, funnelling you straight into a little chimney which, although it has big holds, might cause a few palpitations and where you may feel the time is right to practise your bum-friction technique. Happily, there is no need to consider bequeathing your boots yet as this chimney is avoidable on easier ground just to the right. More rocky steps follow, with further opportunity to refine your slithering skills, but they are quite easy so long as they are taken steadily, then slabby rocks and scree complete the descent to the col at Dore Head.

The drama is all over, but a pleasant stroll remains, back down the valley beside Over Beck, and soon rejoining the outward route at the ladder-stile below Bell Rib.

Seatallan beyond Middle Fell seen from the Great Door

26. Nether Wasdale

Best Map: OS 1:25 000 Outdoor Leisure 6, South
   Western area

Distance: About 4 miles/6.4km

Highest elevation reached: 230ft/70m

Height gained: About 100ft/30m

Star rating: * * *

Level of exertion: Low

Time for the round: About 2 hours

Terrain: Almost all on good paths or tracks.

This splendid walk is almost entirely on the level and increasingly discloses one of the finest panoramic mountain landscapes in the Lake District.

Just east of the hospitable Strands Hotel in Nether Wasdale is a little triangle of roads (grid ref 128038) and easy parking will be found along the edge of one of these. From the north-west point of the triangle take the bridleway, signed for Gill and Buckbarrow, leading north-east. In three hundred yards, the track crosses a little packhorse bridge over a stream, passes between the buildings at Mill Place and then leads across grazing land scattered with fine oak, birch and ash trees. Already the shapely mountains of Buckbarrow, Middle Fell, Yewbarrow, Great Gable and Lingmell are coming into view, as is the superb wall of the Wastwater Screes.

Reaching a wall corner, there is a parting of ways. Take the path to the right signed 'Bridleway Buck Barrow', keeping north-east and almost immediately crossing the tiny stone Scale Bridge. In only a hundred paces beyond it, no more, turn right (south-east, 'bridleway' sign) across more pasture and enter a short walled lane at a gate. This leads to another gate and then across open land beside a wire fence to one more gate with a step-stile. Revert to the north-easterly direction now, following the 'Bridleway Greendale' sign, rising gently across open pasture. The view forward now expands to show the whole cirque of fells around Wasdale Head; only Wastwater is missing and that will soon appear.

Leave the bridleway at a finger-post 'To the lake', and curve across pasture to a ladder-stile at the north corner of High Birkhow Wood and into a lane with a particularly high wall on the left; this surrounds what used to be the kitchen garden for Wasdale Hall, now a Youth Hostel. About a century ago Wasdale Hall was owned by one John Musgrave who also owned land at Seathwaite in Borrowdale. He reckoned that a road

The idyllic head of Wastwater seen from near High Birkhow

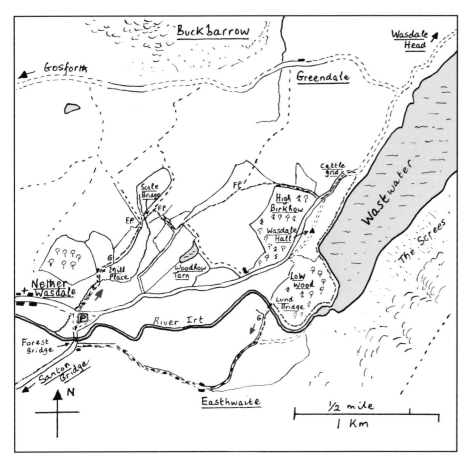

over the Styhead Pass would bring prosperity to his estates on both sides and set about recruiting support for the idea, which would also commemorate the sixtieth anniversary of Queen Victoria's reign. The Highways Board of the time was not prepared to fund the project and public subscription failed to do any better although the plan sputtered along in different forms for several more years including a project for trams up Borrowdale as far as Seascale. Fortunately nothing came of any of it.

Turn left on reaching the road and continue a short distance until just beyond the cattle-grid ahead, when you turn right to cross a stile and follow the permissive path along the lakeshore of Wastwater. Before you do, climb up onto the common on the left of the road for one of the finest classic mountain panoramas in the Lake District; what a wonderful sight!

The lakeshore path soon passes below splendid mature beech trees which ornament the grounds of what must be one of the most beautifully situated Youth Hostels in the country, with the sight of the Wastwater Screes sweeping into the lake becoming more dramatic still, until suddenly the path burrows into a leafy tunnel that persists until it curves around the southern tip of Low Wood and reaches Lund Bridge. Cross the River Irt here and go through a field gate opposite, heading south-west towards the farm at Easthwaite, with a wall on your right. You soon enter a walled lane leading to the farm. The farm track then continues to the road at Forest Bridge and a right turn over this leads back to the car.

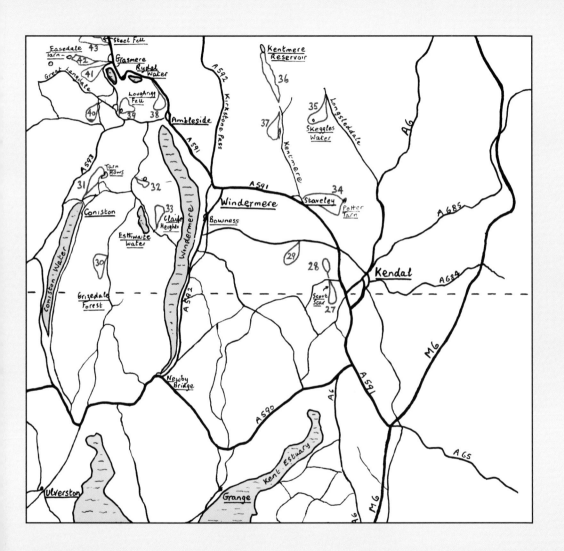

PART TWO

Walks in the
South-East

27. Scout Scar and Sizergh Castle

Best Maps: OS 1:50 000 Landranger 97 Kendal to Morecambe; or
1:25 000 Outdoor Leisure 7, South Eastern area has the first half of the walk only; the southern part is on Pathfinder 627 Milnthorpe

Distance: 4¾ miles/7.6km or 7½ miles/12km if extended to Sizergh Castle

Highest elevation reached: 751ft/229m

Height gained: About 450ft/137m

Star rating: * * / * * *

Level of exertion: Fairly low

Time for the round: About 2½ hours; about 4 hours for the extended walk.

Terrain: All on good paths and tracks.

East of Kendal the land rises in a slope criss-crossed by limestone walls but there is no hint of the limestone escarpment of Scout Scar overlooking the Lyth Valley until you reach it. It gives a great walk along its crest, which could easily be extended to visit the fortified manor of Sizergh Castle and the attractive little Helsington Church as well.

When entering Kendal from the south, both the A6 (from the by-pass) and the A65 meet at a bridge over the River Kent before going into the town centre where a major one-way traffic system operates. At the first set of traffic lights after the bridge turn left up Gillingate and then, half way up the hill and having crossed two transverse roads, turn left up Greenside on the Underbarrow road, which is signed. This crosses the A591 to reach a National Trust car park in an old quarry at the top of the hill (grid ref 488925.) Turn right out of the car park, cross the road to a gate, then a path leads uphill to the escarpment, which drops away into extensive woods but from where there are views as far as Ingleborough, the Howgills, Morecambe Bay and the Lakeland peaks. Walking south along the grassy crest, a four-sided shelter with an iron canopy is soon reached; inside its circular rim is what was once a view indicator giving bearings and distances to many hills and landmarks all around the compass. Vandals have defaced it, so much of the work of identification has now to be imagined.

It is easy walking now along the escarpment, passing by a place marked on the map as 'Hodgson's Leap', which appears to be where the edge is cut by a gully. The trig point is hardly noticed away on your left, until the edge fades and a transverse wall is reached. Veer right here to a gate and a sign 'National

Looking north along Scout Scar

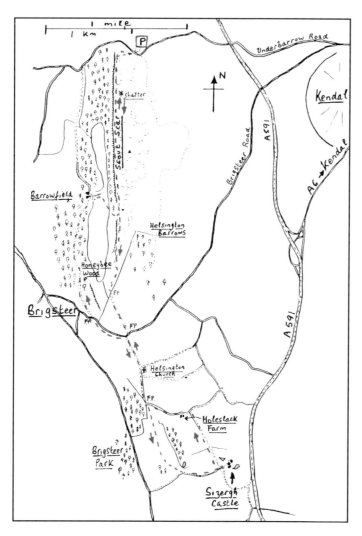

Trust Helsington Barrows'. The path across this attractive heath soon reaches the Kendal–Brigsteer road (grid ref 487893). To return to the start from here, turn downhill for a short way towards Brigsteer, to a track and cattle-grid on a sharp bend, signed for Barrowfield. The track leads through Honeybee Wood, below the Scout Scar escarpment, to reach Barrowfield Farm. From here a finger-post signs the way back up to the escarpment, a narrow path leading up through trees to regain its top again. An easy return is now made along the edge to the car park.

For those wishing to visit Sizergh Castle, turn downhill at Brigsteer Road but then immediately left on a track signed for Helsington Church. This is very tiny but has a fine timber roof and surprisingly, for such a small place, had its own incumbent for 250 years until 1978. Leaving the church, continue south, turning right when the track forks, signed for Brigsteer Park. Beyond a gate, a grassy track leads by the edge of a wood to another gate, then across attractive parkland. To the left (east), the square towers and chimneys of Sizergh Castle come into view and are easily reached by a track which leads into a walled lane. The castle, which is now owned by the National Trust, is frequently open to the public.

To return home, re-enter the lane by which you reached the castle but turn right at a gate and a path then leads across fields to Holeslack Farm. Continuing past this, going north-west, Helsington Church is soon reached again and then the Brigsteer Road. Complete the walk as described above.

28. Cunswick Scar and Tarn

Best Map: OS 1:25 000 Outdoor Leisure 7, South
   Eastern area

Distance: About 3½ miles/5.6km

Highest elevation reached: 679ft/207m

Height gained: About 350ft/107m

Star rating: */* *

General level of exertion: Low

Time for the round: About 2 hours

Terrain: Almost all on firm grassy paths.

To the west of Kendal the land rises gently with little indication that it suddenly terminates in the abrupt limestone edge of Scout Scar. Cunswick Scar is the continuation northwards of that same escarpment and although less defined it still gives a very pleasant easy walk with fine views.

The approach is the same as for Scout Scar (see Walk 27), driving out of Kendal on the Underbarrow road until it crosses the A591 by-pass. At the top of the rise beyond it passes a radio mast, reaching a signed National Trust car park in an old quarry just round a bend in the road (grid ref 988425). However, just before reaching this, there is good parking on a sloping limestone pavement on the right of the road, by a finger-post sign: 'Permissive footpath Cunswick Fell'.

As I got out of my car and put my two miniature Schnauzer dogs on a lead, a lady with two of the same breed walked out of the nearby wood and saw us. Without any hesitation at all she walked straight over saying 'Henry and Freddie, I presume.' She was, of course, right and had seen an illustration of my two dogs and told me that was why she had bought her own. Like dog lovers everywhere, we had a chat, boring to everybody else, I expect, before we parted. I went past the radio mast and took the path into the wood as far as a kissing-gate, and then followed signs alongside a wall, turning east, to reach a four-way sign at the point where the path crosses the cart-track of Gamblesmire Lane. Go due north now on springy turf (signed 'Cunswick Fell') beside the wall enclosing Scar Wood. When the wall ends, a wire fence replaces it and a gate is soon reached where the path turns down into the woods surrounding the almost hidden Cunswick Tarn. Before going into the woods, continue along the edge, now much sharper and more visible and complete the gentle ascent to a large cairn

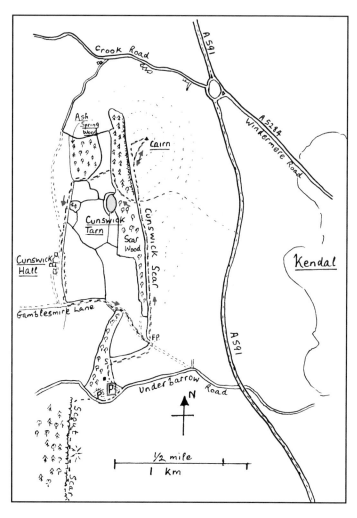

on the highest point of Cunswick Fell, from where there are good views to most of Lakeland's higher fells to the north and west.

Returning now to the gate through the fence, a few steps lead steeply down into the wood, going towards the north-east edge of Cunswick Tarn. This is on private land and not directly accessible, but has reedy margins fringed by willows, alders, silver birch and hazel and is home to many moorhens. The path leads briefly away from the tarn to a kissing-gate and then west across sheep pasture, where in spring I was delighted to see lambs wearing little plastic protective coats. Also here are traces of the foundations of an ancient fortified camp (marked on the map as 'pillow mounds'). The path goes to a gateway at the corner of Ash Spring Wood and the farm track just beyond leads south to join the metalled drive leading past the grey stone buildings of Cunswick Hall. Look particularly for the Royal Arms, the lion and the unicorn carved in a stone above the entrance to the courtyard, for Henry VIII is reputed to have stayed here while courting Catherine Parr, who lived in Kendal Castle.

Before entering the farmyard, go through a gate directly opposite the house, turn right immediately through a kissing-gate and then along the edge of the field (due south) to link up with Gamblesmire Lane at its far end. Turn left, south-west, and this soon leads back up the fields to the four-way signpost and the outward route again.

Looking down on Cunswick Tarn from Cunswick Scar

29. Lord's Lot from Crook

<table>
<tr><td>Best Map:</td><td>OS 1:25 000 Outdoor Leisure 7, South Eastern area</td></tr>
<tr><td>Distance:</td><td>About 5½ miles/8.8km</td></tr>
<tr><td>Highest elevation reached:</td><td>About 675ft/206m</td></tr>
<tr><td>Height gained:</td><td>About 660ft/201m</td></tr>
<tr><td>Star rating:</td><td>*/* *</td></tr>
<tr><td>Level of exertion:</td><td>Low/medium</td></tr>
<tr><td>Time for the round:</td><td>About 3 hours</td></tr>
<tr><td>Terrain:</td><td>Mostly on good paths and tracks although some are not very clear on the ground.</td></tr>
</table>

This low-level walk in the lightly wooded, undulating and tranquil foothills south-east of Bowness crosses arable land, descends gently to the lovely valley of the River Gilpin, then on the return journey traverses some surprisingly wild higher land.

Start just west of the village of Crook, 2 miles/3.2km south of Staveley, at a public footpath sign and gate (grid ref 452951) about a hundred paces east of St Catherine's Church. A couple of cars can park here. A track beyond the gate leads SSW towards a tall tower, soon reached by keeping right (but keep left of the wall ahead) when the track forks. This edifice is a former bell-tower. It is all that remains of the ancient St Catherine's Church and, since a wide crack split its front (unfortunately rather like the Church of England itself), its future looks distinctly shaky.

Continue SSW, with a wall on the left, to reach a slit-stile in a wall-corner; only a hundred paces on the other side turn right (south-west) on a grassy track beside a hedge but then across open field to reach a gate and bridge, where a little stream flowing down the wooded valley on the left is crossed. With the wall beyond on your right, you shortly pass a public footpath sign pointing south-east to Low Fold, worth noting because you will return from there to it. Keep on up the field until it reaches a walled lane with a sign on the immediate left for Birk Moss (farm). A good track leads round to the farm and, directed by arrow signs, a footpath is diverted round it onto a grassy track, still heading south-west. This quickly leads to a high point with a delightful view down a long slope of grass and rocks to the almost secret wooded valley of the River Gilpin. A faint track leads down this to a gate at the entrance to a slutchy walled lane (just south of the place marked Hart Howe on the OS map) and then continues down fields, curving

The descent to the River Gilpin

109

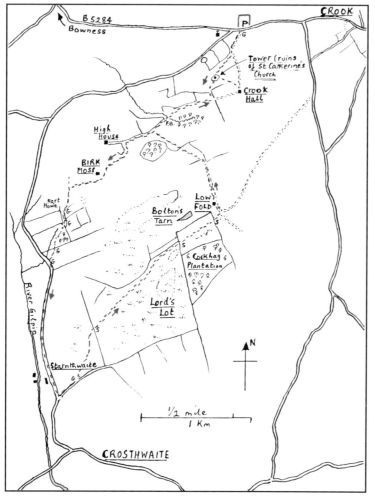

right round a bank and then left at the lower level beside a little beck to a gate. complete the descent down the field, passing a tiny waterfall, to reach another gate and a metalled road (grid ref 435931).

Turn left (south) and go gently downhill along this quiet by-road, passing Starnthwaite Gill, previously a remand home for boys (marked on the OS map as 'Starnthwaite Ghyll School') but now an attractive residential development. Just beyond, as the road rises out of the dip at its lowest point, turn left along a rough track signed 'Public footpath Low Fold'. Quite soon there is a gate and footpath sign on the left and from here, on paths that initially need the eye of faith to discern, head NNE up tree-scattered fields to reach a stile and gate at a fence (grid ref 439925). The path, now traceable, rises up pasture land and then through rocky outcrops profusely covered in yellow gorse in spring and summer, towards a low col just left of the wilderness of Lord's Lot, seen ahead to the right. It reaches open heath scattered with occasional larches and then largely disappears again, but a stile and gate on the top of a little ridge at the north-west corner of Cockhag Plantation soon get you back on course.

Passing just east of the reedy Bolton's Tarn the way leads down a long field to an obvious ladder-stile over a wall and the farm track into Low Fold Farm. Follow the track to the north-west until it fizzles out in a field and then climb another ladder-stile at the edge of a plantation. Just beyond you will see the finger post I mentioned on the outward journey and you can easily return to the start.

30. Carron Crag, Grizedale Forest

Best Map: OS 1:25 000 Outdoor Leisure 7, South Eastern area

Distance: About 3 miles/4.8km

Highest elevation reached: 1030ft/314m

Height gained: About 700ft/213m

Star rating: *

Level of exertion: Fairly low

Time for the round: About 2 hours

Terrain: On forestry tracks and paths, some can be quite muddy.

Grizedale Forest Park, east of Coniston Water, is well promoted by the Forestry Commission (which shows what they can do if they make a bit of an effort) and visitors to the Lake District can hardly fail to be aware of its remarkable Sculpture Trails or the Theatre in the Forest, with its constantly changing repertoire. The Forest Park seems to be enormously popular with mountain-bikers who love getting lost in the maze of tracks. The snack and shopping facilities certainly make it a good venue, even for keen walkers who would normally scorn such blandishments, on a day of poor or indifferent weather.

If you look east from the Visitor Centre (grid ref 335945), where there is parking at a price, you can just see a little outcrop of crags on the skyline and peeping over the trees. This is Carron Crag. The walk circles towards it in an anti-clockwise direction and some of the paths used, marked and signed by the Forestry Commission, are not shown on the OS map, which may be an irritation to those who, like me, like to know precisely where they are all the time.

From the Visitor Centre, go into the large walled conservation nursery (next to the Theatre in the Forest), out through a door in the south wall (on the left) onto a metalled track. Turn right here (SSW), crossing Grizedale Beck and reaching a junction 150 paces past Home Farm. Take the broad path, signed 'Public Footpath Coniston Water 3' to the south-west which, since the Forestry Commission and the Ordnance Survey evidently do not talk to each other, you will not find marked on the OS map. This climbs steadily up a slaty bed amidst mature trees, then swings right (north-east) to join a major forest track. Turn right along this and you will shortly see one of the remarkable forest sculptures, a giant spider in a web; however, you will have just passed the minor track, or path, slanting off left, which you now need.

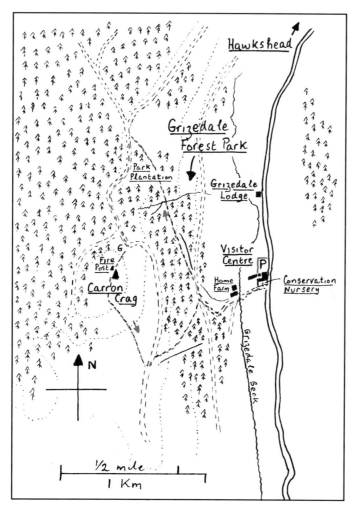

This rises steadily, with a wall on the right, through larches and other conifers, with occasional glades of sycamore and silver birch. When the wall ends, the path carries on to ford a little stream in a dip and reaches another major forestry track (at grid ref 326953 – just north-west of where it says 'Park Plantation' on the OS map if you want to check where you are now. There is a further junction of such tracks just ahead). Turn left (south) here, or you could finish up in Hawkshead.

This broad track climbs gently until, at a fork, you can see ahead the craggy top of Carron Crag, with a fire-observation post on the highest ground. Keep left at the fork and then a gate on the bend ahead leads to a short climb to the top. For the first time, you are really out in the open and can scan a wide expanse of countryside, although you cannot see Coniston Water which is screened by an intervening ridge.

A well-used, though boggy path now descends to the south and can be seen curving away to the south-east to connect with a main forestry track. When reached, go along this, but only for fifty paces as a path turns back sharp left (north-east), with a wall alongside for a short way. This path soon re-enters the forest, gently descending to reach the first main track near the spider sculpture from where you just reverse the first part of the outward walk. You will have had a day with a difference.

Sculptures at the Grizedale Forest Park: left the Woodsman at the entrance to the Centre and right the Spider

31. The Tarns of Tarn Hows from Coniston

Best Map: OS 1:25 000 Outdoor Leisure 7, South Eastern area

Distance: About 6 miles/9.6km, or 4¼ miles/ 6.8km if the circuit of the tarns is omitted

Highest elevation reached: About 850ft/259m

Height gained: About 700ft/213m

Star rating: * * / * * *

Level of exertion: Low

Time for the round: About 3½ hours, or 2½ hours for the shorter walk

Terrain: Almost all on good paths or tracks.

The delightful area of Tarn Hows is rightly loved, with a very short walk starting from near Yew Tree Tarn and then rising beside the beck up Glen Mary being perhaps the most favoured. Even motorists can visit Tarn Hows by car on a one-way road system, with the consequence that it can become a little too popular. This longer walk, however, starts from Coniston and passes through an equally attractive landscape, so that you do not feel any necessity to circuit the tarns themselves when you get there. It makes good use of several National Trust paths not clear on the OS map and is an excellent all-weather and much less-used alternative.

Park in Coniston, or beside the road at Shepherd Bridge where the walk begins (grid ref 305978) at a finger-post. Cross the bridge, turn left (stiles) and then a footpath rises gently to the north-east across pleasant parkland, passing a curious ruin, a high slate wall with tower-like additions at each end. Beyond a gate, continue up a tongue of land with many gorse bushes, to pass through a narrow neck of woods connecting Back Guards Plantation with Guards Wood. More open country follows, with views to the often dramatic waterslide of White Gill draining the Yewdale Fells, then yellow arrows point down a field, through a gate and across another field to go left at a hedged lane which leads beside the Yewdale Beck to the stone bridge at Low Yewdale Farm.

Do *not* cross the bridge here but take the stile and path on the right bank of the beck, soon entering Tarn Hows Wood, an attractive mixture of birches, oaks and conifers. The path rises to the north-east, skirts leftwards round a deer-fenced spruce plantation and then, on a wider track, climbs up on the edge of the woodland, with views down to High Yewdale Farm, to reach Tarn Hows Cottage. The drive from

Tarn Hows in the early evening, with Coniston Old Man in the distance

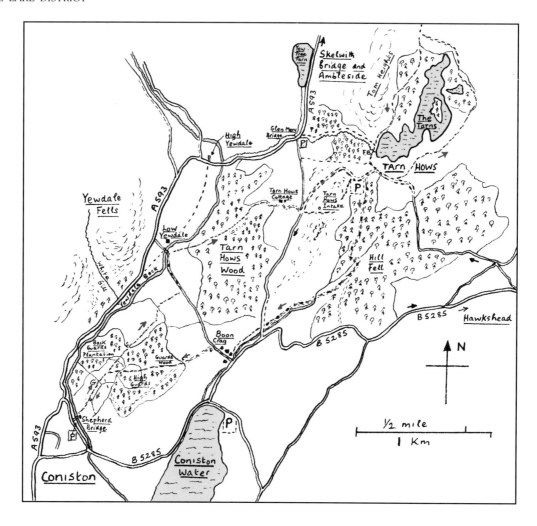

the cottage (signed for Tarn Hows) now winds round a shoulder of fell to join the one-way road system at a gate.

Walk up the tarmac if you like; it's more interesting to cross the road and go steeply up a grassy path through bracken, climbing onto Tarn Hows Intake, an attractive plateau of scattered larch trees and craglets, soon reaching the main Tarn Hows National Trust car park (grid ref 326996). The circuit of the tarns needs no detailed description since it is both well-signed and well-used, but it does visit a fine combination of linked tarns and beautiful trees, with views to the higher surrounding fells.

To return to Coniston, go back to the car park and then south (footpath sign) down the track on its east edge. This soon becomes a delightful ride through mixed woodland covering Hill Fell, gradually descending a wooded valley. Having crossed the beck at the head of a gorge, the track continues easily to a minor road and then a National Trust path enables you to reach the buildings at Boon Crag. A right turn here and then a left at a gate and stile leads up a grassy track to a gate at the entrance to Guards Wood. Just inside you will find an NT sign recommending a way-marked path to Coniston that rises over High Guards and then descends to a stile on the edge of the gorse-covered tongue of land that you crossed on the way out. Turn left (south-east) here and the way home will be obvious.

The Yewdale Fells and Holme Fell seen from near Guards Wood

32. Latterbarrow from Outgate

Best Map: OS 1:25 000 Outdoor Leisure 7, South
    Eastern area

Distance: About 4¼ miles/6.8km

Highest elevation reached: 800ft/244m

Height gained: About 600ft/183m

Star rating: * *

Level of exertion: Medium

Time for the round: About 2½–3 hours

Terrain: Plenty of variety: grassy paths, a little
    tarmac, forest paths and good tracks.

Latterbarrow is a rounded and lightly-wooded hill, well known as a fine viewpoint over Windermere. Often approached from Hawkshead, it is scenically more interesting to go from Outgate, a charming hamlet with a pub of the same name, 1½ miles/2.4km north of Hawkshead. After climbing Latterbarrow this walk could be curtailed but I suggest an entertaining extension into the dense conifer forest, like no fellwalking you have ever done before, and a return across more pleasant parkland.

If patronising the pub, you could no doubt use its car park; otherwise a few cars can be parked on the road opposite, signed 'Barngates' (grid ref 354997). From the pub walk towards Ambleside (north) to a metalled drive on the right with a footpath sign. At its end, a gate leads into a steeply sloping field, from where Latterbarrow can be seen across the intervening valley; then the path goes down the field, crosses a stream and up the slope to a ladder-stile over a wall. Curving leftwards round the hillside, cross a fence by a stile, then follow the farm track towards High Tock How, from where there is a good view over elegant parkland to Blelham Tarn. Turn right at a gate just before the farm and follow a signed path up the field to a gate adjacent to Hole House Farm. Turn south along the farm track and continue along the normally quiet road beyond until, at a gate on the left, there is a National Trust sign for Latterbarrow.

A good path now leads forward up an easy slope; when it forks, take the left-hand one which gives a steep way uphill, trending right as the angle eases to reach the obvious square obelisk, about twice the height of a man, on the summit and which can be clearly seen from the other side of Lake Windermere. It is a superb viewpoint for many if distant hills and a few minutes can be spent trying to identify them

Latterbarrow seen across Blelham Tarn

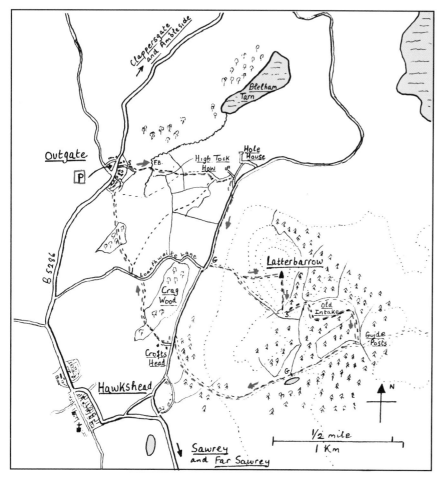

before walking a few paces to the south-east along a grassy ridge. This will enable you to get out of the way of the school parties and see a fine view over the northern end of Windermere.

Leave the top down the slope to the south and, on reaching the wall, step over a stile in the corner and take the path to the left (north-east) along the edge of a larch plantation. It soon zigzags through a wide gap in a wall surrounding 'Old Intake' after which white-topped posts mark a way through a dense conifer wood, with several changes of direction and one short but sharp descent followed by an upward slope, to reach a wall corner and 'Guideposts'. Thank goodness one of these points right (south-west) along a bridle-way to 'Hawkshead'; your exact position would be very uncertain otherwise. This leads through several clearings, with occasional views to the Coniston Fells, passes a small tarn on the left and then winds down through parkland, to meet the road at a gate.

Turn left now along the Hawkshead road but then immediately right down a little lane to Crofts Head. From here a path goes through the tall oaks of Crag Wood, then across open grassland again to a gate into Loanthwaite Lane. Turn left here and just beyond the farm buildings ahead is a sign to the right for 'Outgate and High Wray'. The path forks almost immediately, that on the left leads across lovely parkland (marker-posts), through a small wood and then trends across more pasture to kissing-gates leading into the pub car park at Outgate. It's a handy place to finish an enjoyable walk.

33. The Tarns of Claife Heights from Far Sawrey

Best Map: OS 1:25 000 Outdoor Leisure 7, South
    Eastern area

Distance: About 5 miles/8km

Highest elevation reached: 886ft/270m

Height gained: About 650ft/198m

Star rating: */* *

Level of exertion: Medium

Time for the round: About 3–3½ hours

Terrain: Good tracks on open ground, but much
    stepping over tree roots and diving down dark
    tunnels in the forest. Quite an adventure . . .

Claife Heights is an area of undulating land between Windermere and Esthwaite Water, whose natural woodlands have been almost engulfed by conifer plantations. It does, however, have several delightful man-made tarns, happily in open grazing land. The walk described visits these first; you may return the same way if the walking through the forest is not to your liking. I do urge you to at least sample it. Apart from the much shorter section of forest described in Walk 32 this is like nothing you will ever meet on the open fell and the whole walk turns into a real adventure.

Far Sawrey is at the south end of Esthwaite Water and parking is possible (for a donation in the box) in the grounds of Sawrey Village Hall (grid ref 379954), almost opposite the Sawrey Hotel. Now walk north-west towards Near Sawrey, past the hotel, for about 100 paces and turn off right on a metalled drive. A rougher bridleway soon slants left off this, crosses the Wilfin Beck by a footbridge and then rises gently up a walled and fenced lane through parkland, that mixture of pasture and mature trees that is particularly English. Moss Eccles Tarn is soon revealed over a slight rise, a placid lakelet fringed by alders.

The track is now unwalled, undulating over well-cropped turf with little outcrops and occasional trees, but there is nothing dramatic until, up a little rise, you reach a gate and there is the wonderful view of Wise Een Tarn, forming a foreground to the great fells at the head of Langdale. There will be no better view on this journey.

Still in the open, the track passes a small tarn, rises up more pasture and then enters a plantation at a gate. Passing the overgrown High Moss Tarn, the track becomes a firm forestry road. Stay on it as it

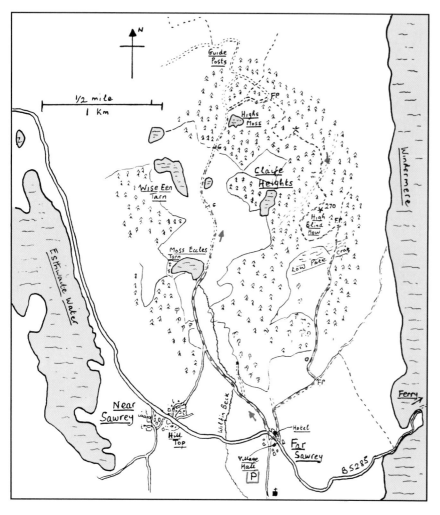

turns downhill to a junction (grid ref 377983) where there is a finger-post signed 'Footpath Far Sawrey'. This is a genuine footpath, leading into spruce woods, picking a way over tree roots and frequently going through dark tunnels between the trees. There are also white-topped marker posts and they are, thankfully, completely reliable; without them, you would soon feel like Hansel and Gretel. They lead round three sides of a rectangle, climb to some bare rock on a much-restricted 'viewpoint', from where you will see a lot more forest but also some sky. You will now cross boggy bits on duckboards, dive into more tunnels and, hooray!, reach a firm track. Turn right (south) here but almost immediately off into forest again at a finger-post 'Footpath Far Sawrey' (grid ref 383976). Another 'viewpoint' on High Blind How (spot height 270m) is reached, then dive into more timber, again go round three sides of a rectangle, again cross a track and beyond it climb up a bank to find a finger-post that says 'Ferry'. Quelling rising panic you walk north-east, passing another 'Ferry' sign; which will give you more palpitations because you know perfectly well that you don't want a ferry, then with relief reach another finger-post, this time reading 'Far Sawrey' and pointing south. The path reaches open glades and then pasture and the path becomes a good track. Turn right just after passing a tiny circular tarn (grid ref 382962) and a pleasant walled lane leads downhill to the road beside the Sawrey Hotel again.

Wise Een Tarn, with Crinkle Crags and Bowfell on the skyline

34. Potter Tarn and the River Kent from Staveley

Best Map: OS 1:25 000 Outdoor Leisure 7, South
　　Eastern area

Distance: About 5 miles/8km

Highest elevation reached: 820ft/250m

Height gained: About 675ft/206m

Star rating: **

Level of exertion: Medium/low

Time for the round: About 2½–3 hours

Terrain: Generally on good paths which may be
　　rather faint on grassy fell near Potter Tarn.

Potter Tarn lies in a fold of land east of Staveley at the southern end of the broad ridge between Longsleddale and the lower valley of the River Kent. This most enjoyable walk rises over undulating land to visit the tarn, descends an attractive gill and then rambles back along a delightful stretch of the River Kent used by the Dales Way.

Parking used to be a nightmare in Staveley but the by-pass changed all that and there is little difficulty in fiding a place nowadays; for instance, on the roadside before it narrows to go up the Kentmere valley (grid ref 470986). Walking north from here up the Kentmere road, turn right at Barley Bridge, where there is a weir across the River Kent. Turn right and then immediately left between houses to see a line of gates and stiles beside a wall rising up the grassy hillside to the north-east. A fine stand of beech trees is passed on the brow of the hill, then more close-cropped fields lead down to Littlewood Farm where, turning right, a metalled track is briefly followed to where a public footpath is signed left down the farm track to Birk Field. Yellow arrows lead round the buildings, then take the grassy path along the valley bottom for a short way before turning up stonier fellside. The path is indistinct in places but Potter Tarn is soon found just over a little rise. It is dammed at the south-east end, originally to create power for paper-mills in Burneside, but is now just a quiet sheet of water visited by a few birds and guarded by sheep.

Cross the wall running south from the tarn by a ladder-stile to the breach in the dam and then turn down a grassy path beside the little stream outflow. This path passes a reed-filled pond on the right and then passes Ghyll Pool, where the stream is again dammed; the path now becomes a grassy track along the top edge of a wooded gill leading south. When this meets a wall and the track forks, turn right (south-west) through a gate and down a narrow

The River Kent near Hagg Foot

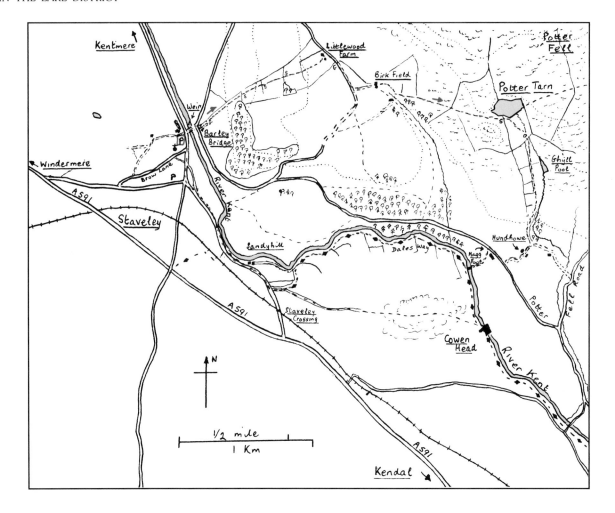

snicket (becoming a walled lane) to reach the various buildings at Hundhowe. The track from here leads obviously to Potter Fell Road.

Turn right now and immediately past the house and farm at Hagg Foot a footpath sign points left between farm buildings and down to a bridge across the River Kent. The footpath of the Dales Way is on the far bank while on this bank is a sign erected by the Woodland Trust inviting visitors to walk in the woods here. My dog Freddie saw cows on the far bank and quietly decided, having had bad experiences with cows, to accept the invitation. I crossed with my other dog and enjoyed the delightful path by the river, winding through a little gorge where there are clear pools followed by rapids where water flows over rocky sills, walking for a considerable distance before I realised there was a dog shadowing me on the far bank. He wouldn't swim for it, he never will, and so I had to return to the bridge, coax him across and then had the pleasure of walking this stretch again. It was no hardship since the gorge is followed by green pastures sweeping down to the south bank and the northern one is clothed with woods. Darting birds fill the air with their song and it is all over too quickly as the path funnels into a walled lane ending at Sandyhill Farm. Before reaching the farm, follow the new signs for the Dales Way which has been re-routed to reach the road just north of Staveley (level) Crossing. An easy stroll beside the road leads back to Staveley.

The weir at Barley Bridge on the River Kent near Staveley

35. Skeggles Water and Longsleddale

Best Map: OS 1:25 000 Outdoor Leisure 7, South Eastern area

Distance: About 6 miles/9.6km

Highest elevation reached: About 1230ft/375m

Height gained: About 700ft/213m

Star rating: *

Level of exertion: Low/medium

Time for the round: About 3½ hours

Terrain: There are good tracks in the valley; on the higher land they are usually grassy, sometimes a bit boggy and sometimes not very obvious.

Lakeland's lower eastern fells are inhabited by curlew and lapwing, grouse and sheep and a few wild horses, as in the Howgills. They are not much visited by humans and a circuit of Skeggles Water can therefore be relied upon to be peaceful when some of the other fells of Lakeland might resemble Blackpool beach. I can't promise anything more exciting than the risk of a sheep stamping its foot at you, but I enjoyed the walk just the same.

There are really only two places to park in Longsleddale. One is at Stockdale (grid ref 492054) where, surprisingly and pleasantly, there is also a little tea-shop. The other is at Sadgill just a little further on, where the metalled road ends and turns over the bridge to the farm and the unmade road continues below Buckbarrow's crags to Haweswater. There is good parking beside the old track (grid ref 483057), but don't obstruct it. I will assume you start the walk from here.

Beyond the bridge, a gate on the left leads into the walled bridleway to Kentmere. This crosses a shallow ford, passes a ruined barn and reaches a six-barred gate. Immediately beyond it, on the left and under trees beside a little stream, is a ladder-stile, from where a path leads down to Till's Hole (farm) and which you would have used if you had parked at Stockdale by following the 'Bridleway Kentmere' sign from the main road opposite Stockdale. Don't use the stile but ford the stream, going forward to another stream and then another gate after which the now faint path curves uphill to the south-west and away from the collapsed wall on the left. When you reach a transverse wall at a breach, don't go through it but turn uphill alongside it, going south-west, onto rough pasture covered in sheep tracks. Keep to the south-west, passing over Cocklaw Fell to reach a substantial

Longsleddale and the hamlet of Sadgill

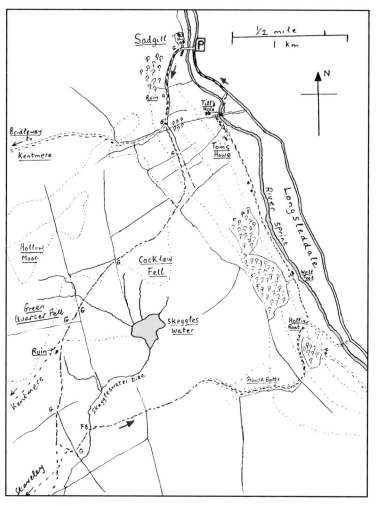

wall pierced by a gate, and here the path becomes clear again. Skeggles Water is now seen down the slope, in a wide and very boggy depression, with reeds on the north side, a solitary rock outcrop, a sole rowan sprouting from a rock and a single hawthorn bush. Fishermen may find the Water of interest but walkers will enjoy it best from the higher, drier land, where the path is.

This continues to two more gates in walls and then reaches a junction of ways close by a ruined building, not much more than a gable end and two walls. The path you need goes south to reach a gate in a wall corner (grid ref 472027) and then continues downhill towards Staveley, intersecting with a rising track heading north-east back onto the higher land again. This is the one you need. Beyond a gate, marker posts show the way to a footbridge over the fast-flowing Skeggleswater Dike; then the path leads back over the highest land, soon becoming an obvious track again which turns towards a wall and then downhill, passing stone grouse butts on the left. The descent to the valley is now obvious, reaching the barns at Hollin Root whose slate roofs are qiute the craziest I have ever seen.

From here, the way leads up the valley, shadowing the River Sprint, a mixture of paths and farm tracks, to join the track to Till's Hole Farm. Turn right here over the bridge across the river, but then sharp left at a gate and alongside the river again to a stile leading into the main valley road. Turn left and Sadgill is now only ten minutes away.

36. The Head of Kentmere

Best Map: OS 1:25 000 Outdoor Leisure 7, South Eastern area

Distance: About 6 miles/9.6km

Highest elevation reached: About 984ft/300m

Height gained: About 430ft/131m

Star rating: *

Level of exertion: Low

Time for the round: About 2½ hours

Terrain: Entirely on good tracks and paths.

This easy and peaceful walk along an almost level valley bottom and through a pastoral landscape leads into the heart of Lakeland's eastern fells. The only parking to be found in Kentmere is about four miles north of Staveley where, after driving through a tunnel of trees, the valley widens a little and the tall square tower of St Cuthbert's Church comes into view. Parking is possible here, next to the church (grid ref 456041) but it will pay to be early. If you are unlucky I suggest you go back to Staveley and try the walk to Potter Fell and the River Kent instead (*see* Walk 34). I may add that I have never failed to find a spot myself, so far.

You may go round the church on either side, heading north-east, onto a track leading first past farm buildings and then, guided by yellow arrows, past Rook Howe and into a walled lane. In about 200 paces pass by a stile on the right leading to a footbridge over the River Kent, to be used on the return, to reach a gate across the lane just beyond. Just thirty paces further, a gate on the left (more arrows) leads into and across a field, heading for the obvious three-stepped profile of Calfhowe Crag seen ahead. Here you join a metalled track and, rounding a wide bend, get your first good view of the high fells at the head of the valley: Yoke, Ill Bell, Froswick, High Street. The tarmac ends at Hartrigg and a good but unsurfaced track now leads forward past a small plantation and with the steep fellside of Rainsborrow Crag directly ahead. This has several belts of vertical rock above extensive screes and was a fashionable rock-climbing ground for a short while until what was then the Lake District's 'current great problem', The Prow, was climbed by Joe Brown. Shortly after that it lapsed into unfashionable obscurity again.

Below and just to the right of the crags, lighter coloured spoil pours out of the mouth of a huge cave and there are several other indications of once exten-

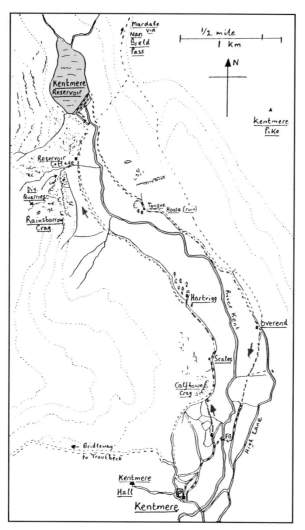

sive quarrying, while ahead can be seen the level line of a green embankment. The track passes Reservoir Cottage and then, rounding a bend, the overflow channel from the Kentmere reservoir is seen. Cross over this by a footbridge and then a footpath takes you to the grassy top of the dam itself; walking along it makes you realise just how much stone went into its construction. The streams from two valleys feed the reservoir and that to the north-east, on the right, leads up to the Nan Bield Pass whose little stone shelter, on the col, can be clearly seen from here on a clear day. I well recall failing to find that pass in a thick mist and descending to the Kentmere reservoir by mistake when my car was parked by Haweswater over the other side. Toiling back over the pass made a memorable experience that I hope not to repeat.

A pleasant path, rather than a track, leads back down the east side of the valley, passing the ruins of a barn beside a small stand of Scots pines and a semi-circular wall sheltering the remains of an earlier settlement. It then becomes a farm track again through numerous fields, with gates, to reach the farm at Overend. Take the lower, right-hand, way here which soon becomes an easy grassy track leading into a walled lane. Look out for a through-stone stile on the right; the path on the other side takes you through trees to the little footbridge mentioned on the out-ward journey. Turn left here and all paths and tracks now lead back to Kentmere Church.

Looking up Kentmere from near Brockstones

37. Whiteside End and Kentmere Tarn

Best Map: OS 1:25 000 Outdoor Leisure 7, South Eastern area

Distance: About 5 miles/8km

Highest elevation reached: About 950ft/290m

Height gained: About 450ft/137m

Star rating: */* * *

Level of exertion: Low

Time for the round: About 2½ hours

Terrain: Almost all walking on good tracks or paths.

Peaceful and pastoral lower Kentmere gives some very attractive walking and this is a good example of it, climbing gently to a shoulder on a grassy fell, descending just as gently to the valley again and returning with a ramble alongside the waters of Kentmere Tarn.

Parking is limited in Kentmere to a few places next to St Cuthbert's Church (grid ref 456041) where the valley briefly widens about four miles north of Staveley. Having arrived there early enough to secure a place, take the walled cart-track leading towards the newer farm buildings attached to the old pele tower at Kentmere Hall; this is typical of the border-country fortified farmhouse, and the tower is still in good condition. From a gate in front of the Hall, a track crosses the beck by a ford and rises gently beside the upper edge of Hall Wood, soon allowing views over the Kentmere valley, to Green Quarter Fell and back to the fine ridge rising towards Kentmere Pike. Still rising, the first track swings west round Whiteside End (a little walk onto the slightly higher Mould Rigg improves the views) then becomes more a grassy path (less used by farm vehicles) and begins a slight descent towards a lightly-wooded gill. Here there is a triangular sheepfold in the wall-corner and a gate, beyond which the grazed pastures end and rougher grass, bracken and rushes take over. Go through the gate but do not cross Park Beck yet; turn instead to the south-east and follow the grassy path to cross the stream a little lower down at a ford. The path leads pleasantly through bracken towards Meadowplatts Plantation, with mature oakwoods on the left hand and a sight of the prominent cairn (Williamson's Monument) on Hugill Fell down the valley.

There is a little stone hut beside the ford used to cross another stream and then the path continues

Looking south from the fellside near Whiteside End

135

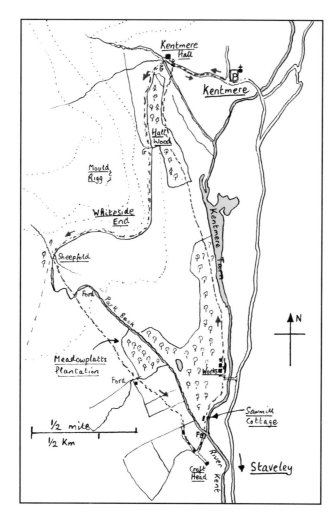

downhill to enter a walled lane at a gate. Just before reaching Croft Head, turn sharp left along another grassy walled lane to reach a gate on the wooded bank of the River Kent. A narrow footbridge crosses Park Beck yet again (which here joins the Kent) and the path leads in front of the attractive Sawmill Cottage and onto its metalled driveway, continuing beside the river to reach some large industrial buildings. They appear to be mostly empty now although diatomite, a mineral used in insulation, was extensively mined here in the past.

When I peered through a window into what looked like an empty interior, I was surprised to see a face peering back at me. I felt I had to say something and so mouthed, 'What do you do here?' He opened the window and gave me the cryptic answer, 'We analyse sand.' Not feeling much wiser, I asked a few more questions but the scientific answers left me even more baffled, so we parted.

The path passes in front of the buildings, then a grassy track leads forwards, with woodlands on the left and, very shortly, the waters of Kentmere Tarn appear on the right. There are very few indications that the waters had their industrial importance too, and I could see no sign of the 'Aerial Ropeway' marked on the map and simply followed a lovely unfenced grass path or track alongside and a little above the level of the peaceful waters. This soon leads into the lower edge of Hall Wood again and then alongside it to a final ford across the beck only a short way from Kentmere Hall where the outward path is rejoined.

38. Lily Tarn on Loughrigg Fell from Rydal

Best Map: OS 1:25 000 Outdoor Leisure 7, South
 Eastern area

Distance: About 3½ miles/5.6km

Highest elevation reached: About 656ft/200m

Height gained: About 500ft/152m

Star rating: * * *

Level of exertion: Low

Time for the round: About 2 hours

Terrain: Good paths throughout.

Lily Tarn is nothing special in itself, just a shallow and largely reed-filled sheet of water, but its situation is what makes it a worthwhile objective. Loughrigg Fell is a mountain range in miniature and although its topography can be very confusing – and not only in mist – it is a delightful place from which to view many surrounding higher fells seen in all quarters of the compass. This short but very attactive walk visits the eastern end of the fell, returning by an intricate way through some lovely deciduous woods, particularly attractive in the spring or autumn.

Start from Rydal (about 1½ miles/2.4km north of Ambleside on the A591) by crossing the bridge at the outflow from Rydal Water, then turning sharp right over the cattle-grid to the car park (grid ref 365059). Now walk along the quiet minor road going south alongside the River Rothay, shortly passing some stepping-stones across it and continuing until a finger-post sign is reached on a bend immediately before a house called Fox Ghyll. A good path turns off the road here, leading beneath some magnificent beech trees and up Fox Ghyll, shortly crossing the beck at a kissing-gate and footbridge, passing through an area rich with rhododendrons, then continuing gently uphill with a wall on the left-hand side.

As the wall turns sharply left round the head of the gill (now little more than a grassy groove) continue just over the broad hause ahead to reach a junction of paths by a tiny tarn (grid ref 356044). The main path continues ahead to the south-west towards Langdale and Skelwith Bridge and you should take it, *but only for ten paces*, no more. Turn off it onto a lesser path, which crosses a tiny stream and leads south, keeping the wall on your right and rising past a triangular-shaped sheepfold in a wall corner. The path now undulates along the ridge, going east, and there are beautiful views to the Fairfield Horseshoe and up

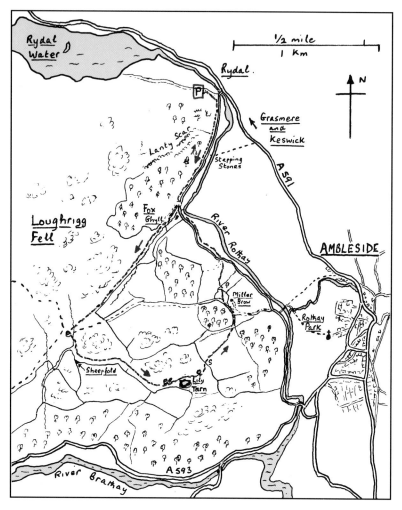

Langdale from several points along it, until you reach two gates ahead separated by a short length of wire fence. Go through either gate; the paths unite again shortly on the far side of the rise ahead, and passes two tiny tarns on the left. Just beyond is the much larger Lily Tarn, about 50 yds/45m in diameter and almost triangular, and from where you can see to Fairfield, and to Ill Bell and Froswick on the long ridge rising to High Street. Continue just a little further to the south-east to the rocky outcrop of Todd Crag (which surely cannot be where the OS have placed it on their 1:25 000 map) for an excellent bird's-eye view over the bustling town of Ambleside.

A hundred paces north-east of Lily Tarn is a much smaller one, very overgrown, and fifty paces beyond that, just over the rise ahead, is a ladder-stile over the wall. The path beyond leads downhill to the north-east to reach a wall-corner at the bottom edge of a wood where it crosses a tiny beck, leads through woodland beyond and descends a little iron-runged ladder to reach a firm track at Miller Brow (grid ref 367045). Now turn left (north-west) along this, but only for 150 paces until it is on the level, then turn off right down a little-used path marked by yellow arrows on posts. These lead through lovely woodland, climbing two walls by ladder-stiles and into an open sloping field and so down to reach the metalled road. Turn left here; you soon pass Fox Ghyll again and rejoin the outward route. A lovely walk.

The stepping-stones across the River Rothay near Fox Ghyll

39. *Little Loughrigg and Loughrigg Fell*

Best Map: OS 1:25 000 Outdoor Leisure 7, South
Eastern area

Distance: About 3½ miles/5.6km

Highest elevation reached: 1099ft/335m

Height gained: About 1060ft/323m

Star rating: * * *

Level of exertion: Medium

Time for the round: About 2½ hours

Terrain: On generally good paths, with a stony
ascent beside a gill to the top of Loughrigg
Fell.

Crinkled, crumpled Loughrigg Fell is ideal for mini-fellwalking and this superb walk visits it once more (*see* Walk 38), this time climbing over Little Loughrigg and passing Loughrigg Tarn as well.

The Silverthwaite car park, found ½ mile/800m past Skelwith Bridge towards Elterwater (grid ref 342037) is marked on the OS map but the footpath leading from it onto Little Loughrigg is not shown at present, so don't let that confuse you. Beside the gate

to the cottage on the corner of the car park, take a footpath heading north beside the wall. It is almost hidden amongst silver birch and bracken and climbs to a ladder-stile at the entrance to a wood. Do *not* cross here but turn right (north-east) up a grassy path to some larches on the skyline ahead from where there is a good view of Loughrigg Tarn. This must be one of the most beautifully situated tarns in Lakeland, backed by fellsides whose lower slopes are wooded and which rise apparently to no fewer than four craggy minor tops, seen from here. Green pastures grazed by cows and sheep lead down to the water's edge, white cottages shelter beneath mature trees and are almost reflected in the placid waters; it is a scene of tranquillity. The path slants across the slope towards two of the cottages at Loughrigg Fold and joins the road, going left for about a hundred paces to a stile and gate on the right. A path from here leads into the picture, across the meadows beside the tarn and then up a short slope to a gate beside farm buildings at The How. Turn left here along this good track, below superb pines, and in about a hundred paces is a gate with a sign 'National Trust Loughrigg Fell' and an arrow pointing left alongside a fence which shortly becomes a wall. A grassy track now slants northwards beside the wall to reach a gate at the foot of a gully.

*Loughrigg Fell and Tarn,
evening*

141

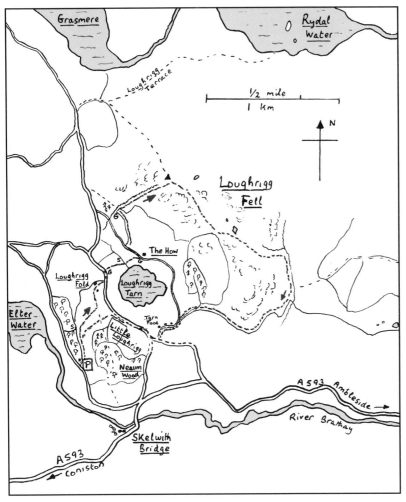

Just before the wood beyond, turn steeply uphill on a path up the gill. A steady ascent soon leads to a hause and the main top with its trig point and panoramic views is found just a little higher to the left.

From the top return to the col and then head south-east, towards Lake Windermere, on the main cairned path down a steep grassy depression. This path undulates, passing a depression on the left containing one or sometimes more shallow and reedy tarns. Don't veer off down brackeny slopes to the right but keep on this main path descending towards Ambleside seen ahead, before joining another major track on a hause, by a little tarn. Swing right (south-west) here and continue the descent, curving round the fell at a lower level and now having lovely views up Langdale. The main intake wall soon comes in on the left and the path runs beside it to a gate on the edge of a little wood after which it winds down to enter a walled lane with a gate at its end.

Here take the right fork, signed 'Langdale', past a house called Dillygarth and then past Tarnfoot Farm next to it. Here go left on the metalled track to a road junction, with a GPO post box in the wall, then right to yet another junction where there is a sign 'High Close and Grasmere' to the right. Next to this is a slate sign saying 'Path to Elterwater/Langdale 330yds'. Turn right along the road and sure enough a grassy path soon veers off the tarmac, goes up the slope beside the wall on the left and rejoins the outward path by the larch trees at the top of the slope. A straightforward descent leads back to Silverthwaite car park.

40. *Sawrey's Wood and Fletcher's Wood*

Best Map: OS 1:25 000 Outdoor Leisure 7, South Eastern area

Distance: About 3½ miles/5.6km

Highest elevation reached: About 625ft/190m

Height gained: About 425ft/130m

Star rating: **/***

Level of exertion: Low

Time for the round: About 2 hours

Terrain: On good paths through woodland and across pasture.

This delightful low-level undulating ramble reveals some splendid views, particularly over Little Langdale. It starts at a pub and there is another halfway; its only drawback is a short walk along tarmac at the end.

Start from Elterwater, where there is a National Trust car park opposite the Britannia Inn (grid ref 328047) or on the edge of the B5343 at Walthwaite Bottom (grid ref 329051). Immediately you have crossed Great Langdale Beck, turn right (north-west) on the metalled track beside the river which, after a little way reaches a point where a footpath is signed down to the river bank. Don't cross the footbridge when it is reached but keep beside the beck until you reach a concrete pump-house where you turn uphill, through a high cutting in a slate tip, to join the quarry road. This is followed into the quarry yard passing several large sheds and then the footpath leads up a rough track to reach a metalled one on the edge of Sawrey's Wood.

Turn right here, but only for fifty paces until directly opposite Crossgates Cottage, where you turn off the road and take a path heading uphill to the SSW, into Sawrey's Wood with its many fine trees. Another broader track (leading up to the old quarries on Lingmoor Fell) is shortly crossed but your path rises ahead, leading into a partly sunken walled lane and, over the top of the rise, to join the main Elterwater–Little Langdale track. About three hundred paces to the right along this is a sign 'Public footpath only' (to make it clear that mountain bikes are not welcome) which leads south across open pasture with scattered trees and fine views to the Coniston Fells. This path descends slightly to two slit-stiles and then down the right edge of a gently sloping field to reach the road at Wilson Place Farm. The Three Shires Inn will be found about 150 paces along the road to the right.

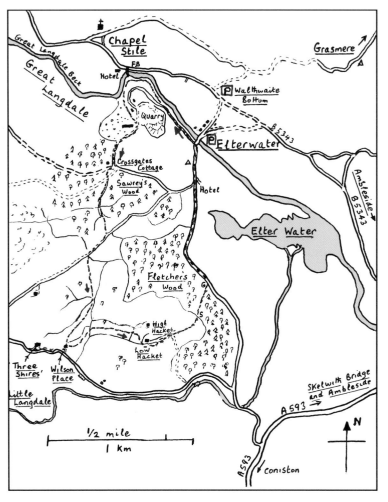

To continue the walk, just before reaching the road turn left (east) to a gate and track beyond leading back uphill, with 'footpath' painted on the left-hand one of two gates ahead. Heading north-east up a walled field to a first stile, then half-right to some steps and stile at another wall, the way now turns east, with little sign of the path, up a long pasture to reach a gateway into the field ahead. Veer right now, to a gate and stile in this field corner after which finger-posts and signs for 'Elterwater' lead you round the house of Low Hacket to its driveway. Two hundred paces past a barn, where the drive swings sharp right, go straight ahead (north-east) signed across more lovely pasture-land leading gently downhill to a stile into Fletcher's Wood.

It was peaceful enough as we neared the stile, and the friendly little donkey grazing in the field allowed my wife to stroke its nose. As we walked away, it craftily sidled close up to Henry, our younger dog, who didn't notice the move and with one lightning stamp squashed him into the turf. Henry squealed, I shouted in alarm and the donkey backed off although it was only waiting a chance for another attack. Fortunately Henry was only bruised and was soon running around again. We needed the peace and calm of this fine mixed wood through which the path leads to recover our own composure and then, reaching the road where we turned left, we were soon back to Elterwater.

Wetherlam peeping over the village of Elterwater

41. Megs Gill and Huntingstile from Grasmere

Best Map: OS 1:25 000 Outdoor Leisure 7, South
    Eastern area

Distance: About 4 miles/6.4km

Highest elevation reached: About 890ft/271m

Height gained: About 950ft/290m

Star rating: **/***

Level of exertion: Low/medium

Time for the round: About 2½ hours

Terrain: On generally good paths; the descent
    alongside Megs Gill is fairly steep.

This is a delightful walk, of varied scenery and with some lovely views, from the Vale of Grasmere over the low ridge separating it from Great Langdale, then back again by a different route.

The centre of Grasmere has become more and more like a shopping mall in recent years but happily it seems the planners have at last recognised this and are now taking steps to hold onto the charm of this lovely village. Unfortunately the developments have led to the most convenient car park for this walk also becoming the most expensive, so it will pay to look around a little further. Having done so, walk out along the Red Bank road, towards Great Langdale. Pass the Gold Rill Hotel, continue round the corner and then take the narrow walled lane opposite the boat landings (gate and 'public footpath' sign). The lane climbs to a kissing-gate, then rises across open pasture, with some superb ice-smoothed *roches moutonnées* on the left of the path, to a second gate.

Continue alongside the wall traversing the rocky lower slopes of Silver How, with a larch wood over the wall on the left, and the path reaches a shoulder where the wall turns noticeably downhill. Don't follow the wall, or turn sharply uphill (which leads to Silver How) but continue ahead. The path still climbs gently up open brackeny slopes dotted with dark juniper shrubs, to reach the crest of the broad grassy ridge and a first view down the other side to Great Langdale, backed by Lingmoor Fell. That's the first puff over.

Paths run along the crest of the ridge in both directions but cross the hause on a narrow path slanting delicately across a steep slope and round towards the waterfalls in Megs Gill, seen directly ahead. Cross the stream on rocky ledges just above the falls, then continue down the right bank of the

Looking down on Chapel Stile from Spedding Crag near Megs Gill

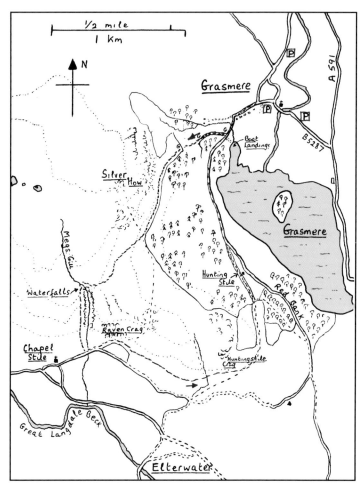

gill to reach the side road just outside the little hamlet of Chapel Stile.

Turn left here, away from the village, but in only fifty paces or so take the green path on the left slanting away from the road ('public footpath' sign) and beside the wall below the steep buttresses of Raven Crag. Years ago, when I was climbing every weekend, I persuaded my (non-climbing) younger brother to accompany me on one of the excellent routes here. He astonished me by swarming up it like a monkey. Ignore the path turning steeply up a shallow gully on the left and stay on the main one alongside the wall, until the wall curves downhill, then continue across the grassy slopes beyond, shadowing the road below.

This path rises gradually across the brackeny fell through an attractive landscape dotted with junipers and hawthorns and becoming rather vague where it traverses a little gill but, just past a small roofless slate building seen directly below, it joins a well-used path rising from Elterwater. Turn more steeply uphill now to the north-east, below the broken rocks of Huntingstile Crag and towards the left-hand end of woods on the skyline ahead. A splendid view of the fells beyond Grasmere is seen as soon as the top of the rise is reached. A delightful descent follows, funnelled between stone walls, to a gate where the path joins the walled lane of the old corpse road leading past the house of Huntingstile and joining the Red Bank road at Lea Cottage. A stroll down the road soon leads back to Grasmere village.

42. Easedale Tarn

Best Map: OS 1:25 000 Outdoor Leisure 7, South Eastern area

Distance: About 5 miles/8km

Highest elevation reached: About 920ft/280m

Height gained: About 800ft/244m

Star rating: * *

Level of exertion: Fairly low

Time for the round: About 2½ hours

Terrain: All on good paths, some rather stony. Stepping-stones at two points could give some quite exciting moments if water levels are high.

The walk to Easedale Tarn from Grasmere is well-loved and well-trodden, gaining height gradually and popular as an all-weather walk through a continually changing landscape. Few walkers, however, seem to know of a much more interesting start (or finish) than the standard one, so the following description may be of interest to those who know the walk already, as well as for newcomers.

Instead of walking out of Grasmere up the Easedale Road, or driving up it and parking (if you are lucky) in the well-signed little car park at grid ref 334080, the way I suggest starts opposite the Red Lion Hotel in the middle of Grasmere (grid ref 336076). From here walk north-west and parallel to Easedale Drive, up a metalled track past the building that was formerly the village's police station (and is marked as such on the OS map). The drive shortly crosses a cattle-grid and then rises towards Allen Bank, the large house occupied for a short time by William Wordsworth. In front of the house the drive swings right and is followed round to some cottages, with good views over to Helm Crag on the way. From here a walled lane leads up towards Lang How while, immediately beyond the cottages, a path signed for Goody Bridge leads north-east down fields to a ladder-stile. Just over the other side are seven or eight stepping-stones across the Easedale Beck, then signs lead up the field, to pass in front of the buildings of Goody Bridge Farm and join the road beyond.

Turn left here (joining the normal route, which is now followed) to where the road bends. Here there is a footbridge on the left and the path to Easedale Tarn is signed across it, thereafter shadowing the line of Easedale Beck across meadows and sheep pastures before climbing beside the waters of the gill to a higher level. The rocks in the bed of the stream, from

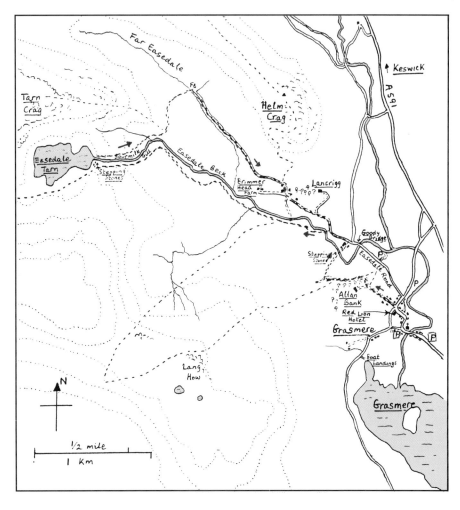

the foot of the falls upwards, give gill-scramblers a few moments of sport if the water is not too high, but after heavy rain they can be completely covered and this little force can turn into a thundering cascade of white water which is of course responsible for its name of Sourmilk Gill.

A last rise across fairly stony ground leads to the outflow from Easedale Tarn and a pleasant picnic spot on the shore in good weather, but as a rule it is the journey rather than the destination that gives this walk its special appeal and few parties linger long, preferring either to extend the walk to Codale Tarn and on to Sergeant Man (turning it into a much bigger expedition) or returning to Grasmere by reversing the approach route.

For a different return and assuming that the water level is not too high, cross the outflow from the tarn on big stones to a footpath on the far bank. This tracks the course of Sourmilk Gill, then curves to the north-east round the toe of the long bracken-covered ridge running down from the heights of Tarn Crag and slants across fellside to a footbridge across the beck flowing down Far Easedale Gill. The path soon runs between stone walls, and past Brimmer Head Farm to the little hamlet at the end of the road. A short walk down this soon leads to Goody Bridge Farm again and you may either reverse the outward walk back over the stepping-stones or simply continue down the road back to Grasmere.

Descending towards Grasmere from near Easedale Tarn

43. Steel Fell and the Greenburn Skyline

Best Maps: 1:50 000 Landranger 90 Penrith,
    Keswick & Ambleside area
    At 1:25 000 scale, both Outdoor Leisure 7,
    South Eastern area, and Outdoor Leisure 4,
    North Western area are needed.

Distance: About 5 miles/8km

Highest elevation reached: 1814ft/553m

Height gained: About 1700ft/518m

Star rating: * *

Level of exertion: Medium

Time for the round: About 3½ hours

Terrain: Good grassy paths on the lower fells,
    boggier and peatier ones on the higher fells.
    The final descent is on steep grass and great
    care is needed if it is wet, although there is an
    easier alternative.

Steel Fell overlooks the Pass of Dunmail Raise where the road leads from Grasmere towards Keswick. From the pass, very steep slopes of scree rise inexorably to a loose gully and easier ground is only reached high above it; the views down, as might be expected, are splendid. Fortunately, it also throws down an inviting grass spur, well seen from both the main road and from Grasmere, which makes for a simple and direct approach, allows excellent views along the pass also and can be followed by a good round of the head of the valley of the Green Burn.

As alternatives to walking from Grasmere you could park just north of the Traveller's Rest on the A591 out of Grasmere towards Keswick, where the road takes a bend. From here (grid ref 336092) a side road turns downhill to cross the River Rothay. Or you could use the car park up Easedale Road out of Grasmere at Goody Bridge (grid ref 334080), adding about 1½ miles/2.4km to the spec above. From either, walk along to Ghyll Foot and then up the gravel drive beyond to a gate just after the last house; here there is a National Trust notice 'Green Burn'.

Immediately through the gate, turn sharp right and follow a lovely green path rising steadily up the obvious grassy ridge. Two gateways lead beyond the intake walls and the path rises steadily until your nose is almost up against a little rock outcrop, skirted on the right. The grassy ridge continues thereafter, overlooking the Dunmail Raise road, to a shoulder from where the Green Burn valley is laid out like

The ridge rising to Steel Fell, from near Grasmere

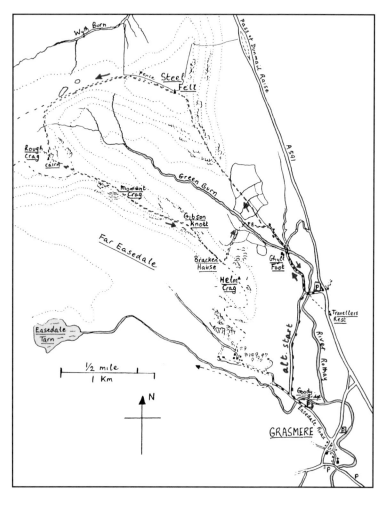

a map below. The path zigzags up another steep section just beyond, then leads out onto a broad grassy top, shortly afterwards reaching a large cairn on Dead Pike, the highest point on Steel Fell.

A path, beside a wire fence, now runs along a broad ridge to the north-west and, when the fence ends, continues in the same direction towards some obvious but unnamed reedy pools on the ridge top from where there are good views to Helvellyn. Old iron fence posts continue the ridge-line from the tarns towards Greenup Edge and the shoe-marks of fell-runners may often be observed in the peaty soil, for this is a linking section of the Bob Graham Round (which aims to cover all the major peaks of the Lake District in 24 hours). Leaving the ridge-line, there is no clear path across the next section at the head of Green Burn because it is rough and inclined to be wet but the objective is an obvious cairn on Rough Crag. Just beyond the cairn, you will pick up the well-used path traversing the Helm Crag ridge and can turn south-east along it, undulating over Moment Crag and then Gibson Knott to reach Bracken Hause, the last col before the climb up to the 'Lion and Lamb' rocks on Helm Crag.

If you are parked at Goody Bridge, the best descent will be down the well-marked and signed path from the top of Helm Crag. If parked near the Travellers Rest, descend steep grass slopes to the NNE to a ladder-stile, to a gate and then to a footbridge which leads across the Green Burn to rejoin the outward route.

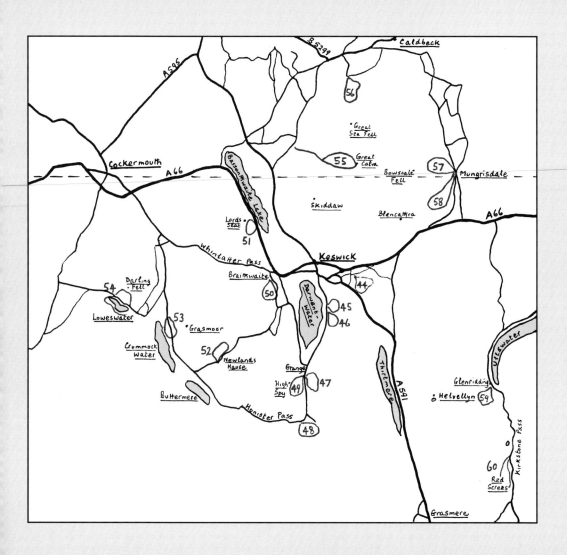

PART THREE

Walks in the North

44. Low Rigg and the Naddle Valley

> **Best Map:** OS 1:25 000 Outdoor Leisure 4, North Western area
>
> **Distance:** About 4 miles/6.4km
>
> **Highest elevation reached:** About 1000ft/305m
>
> **Height gained:** About 525ft/160m
>
> **Star rating:** */ * *
>
> **Level of exertion:** Low
>
> **Time for the round:** About 2 hours
>
> **Terrain:** Easy going (and easy route-finding) on good paths and tracks.

This easy walk rambles over low-level grazing land in a splendid setting of higher fells and is suitable for almost any weather conditions.

There is parking on the road on the north side of the finest stone circle in the Lake District, at Castlerigg outside Keswick (grid ref 292238). Situated in a natural arena of the high fells of Skiddaw, Blencathra and the Dodds Ridge, the forty-eight stones are all of Borrowdale volcanic origin and ten of them form a sanctuary within the larger circle. Two large stones are like gateposts and form a natural entry to it and it is estimated that it was built about 3000 years ago. There are people who believe such sites have connections with lines of natural force or power in the universe; standing here it is fairly easy to see why.

Go east from the car park along the road towards Goosewell Farm to a finger-post signed 'Public footpath The Nest.' A pleasant grassy path now leads roughly south-west across sloping pastures overlooking the Naddle valley and passes a covert of trees that shelters pheasant. Walking over here on a perishing cold December's day I felt sorry for the poor old pheasants being flushed out of their warm roosts by a beater, to face the gauntlet of waiting guns. Then I thought, as I crossed the three ladder-stiles to the gateway at the dwelling of High Nest, how tasty is a bit of pheasant at Christmas. Turn off its drive at a cattle-grid, going left down a field to a stile, by-passing the farm at Low Nest, and then joining the A591 for a few paces to reach a slit-stile on the left.

A signed path now leads south-east down to the valley bottom, over a little beck at a bridge, then turns to the east at a way-marker. A footbridge over the Naddle Beck leads to a gate and across a large field, heading for the obvious broad col between the high land of Low Rigg on the left and the more crinkly and crumpled rocky spine of High Rigg on the right. Cross the track to Sykes Farm and now climb

Low Rigg and Blencathra seen across the Naddle Valley

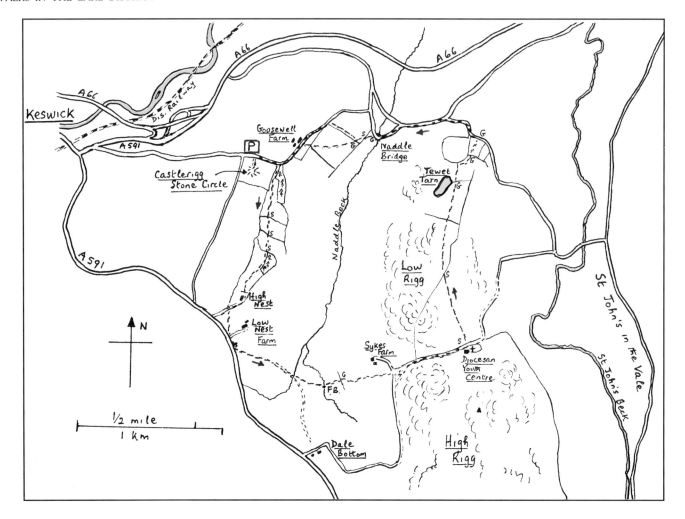

Keswick

A66

A66

A66

Dis. Railway

A591

A591

P

Goosewell Farm

Castlerigg Stone Circle

Naddle Bridge

Tewet Tarn

Naddle Beck

Low Rigg

High Nest

Low Nest Farm

Sykes Farm

Diocesan Youth Centre

N

½ mile
1 km

FB.

Dale Bottom

High Rigg

St John's in the Vale

St John's Beck

the rougher slope of rocky knolls and oak trees beyond to join the partly metalled track leading to the Carlisle Diocesan Youth Centre.

Almost hidden behind this is the tiny church of St John's in the Vale, the supposed site of earlier buildings erected by the Knights Hospitallers of the Order of St John during or after the Crusades. The tiny spring or well of St John may be found in the south-west corner of the churchyard, beneath an ancient yew. An iron goblet chained to the rock beside the spring provided a shelter for a large spider on my last visit.

Directly opposite the church is a slit-stile and from here a green path leads northwards through bracken, by-passing the highest rocky top of Low Rigg to a stile in a transverse wall. Now the land slopes to the north and Tewet Tarn (often covered with ice-skaters' trails in hard winters) is seen ahead. The path leads east of it, through a hurdle gate, then straight ahead, turning right at a wall then downhill through two gates to reach a minor road. A left turn here, also bearing left at the next two junctions, leads to Naddle Bridge. Cross this, then leave the road by a gate on the left leading to a ladder-stile and second gate. Here you will find a sign 'Permissive footpath Castlerigg' which avoids a large field usually full of cows and leads alongside a hedge to the road just north-east of Goosewell Farm. Carry on past this and the car park is just round the corner.

St John's in the Vale Church

45. *Cat Gill and Walla Crag, Borrowdale*

Best Map: OS 1:25 000 Outdoor Leisure 4, North Western area

Distance: About 3 miles/4.8km

Highest elevation reached: About 1240ft/378m

Height gained: About 950ft/290m

Star rating: **/***

Level of exertion: Low/medium

Time for the round: About 2 hours, if you take your time

Terrain: On good paths, stonier and steeper up Cat Gill but generally easy.

Wooded slopes along Derwentwater, rising to open fell, with glorious views over the lake; these are the ingredients for what is a lovely walk at all seasons, but especially in the autumn when the trees are at their best.

Start from the Great Wood car park (grid ref 272213) which is about 1 mile/1.6km out of Keswick along Borrowdale Road. This car park is run by the National Trust and there is now a ticket-machine here strategically placed beside the gate out of the south-east corner, (i.e. top right-hand) so that you won't fail to notice it as you take the track signed 'Ashness Bridge and Walla Crag'. This leads through some superb mature larch, beech and oak trees. When it forks, bear right (signed 'Ashness Bridge'; the other fork is for the return) and take the rising track, which soon allows views over Derwentwater with its wooded islands, until it forks again immediately before reaching the rushing waters of Cat Gill. A footbridge leads across the beck, heading for Ashness Bridge (Walk 46); instead turn along the left bank of the gill on a good path winding up through the trees. Higher up the gill the top rocks of Upper Falcon Crag come into view; whenever I see them, I cannot help but think of the time when I fell into space from the top of its vertical corner. I was roped, of course, and that time my wife held the rope so I was only given a fright. There was an occasion when she didn't, when I was learning the hard way about putting pitons correctly into cracks in rock. One came out, she didn't hold the rope and I landed on my back at the bottom of the quarry. Only just conscious, I saw the faces of two little boys peering over the top. 'Is he dead?' said one. 'No, I don't think so,' said the other. 'Let's bugger off then,' said the first, and they disappeared, whistling cheerfully.

Causey Pike seen across Derwentwater from below Falcon Crag

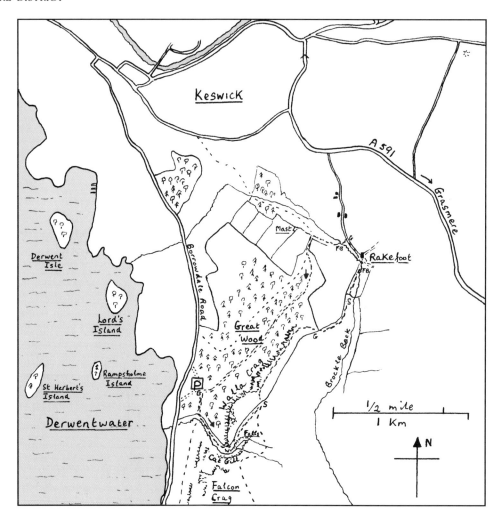

Beyond a kissing-gate, the path zigzags up the flank of the gill, which is still a deep ravine (giving a reasonable gill-scramble, incidentally); then, near its top, there is a pretty waterfall as it forks. Still climbing, but now on a grassy path, you rise above the trees, with the wall on your left side, to reach the open fell. Here there is a stile over the wall, then a delightful path undulates along the top edge of the rocks of Walla Crag, giving more marvellous views over the lake and back up Borrowdale, until it joins a green track, with a wall on the left, leading down now towards the beck in the gill of Rakefoot.

A footbridge over Brockle Beck leads to the farm but just down the lane turn left at a gate leading down to another footbridge, thus re-crossing the beck (finger-post sign 'Springs Farm'). Keep close to the beck for a short way and then pass along the lip of the gill until another kissing-gate is reached, with a sight of a radio mast beyond. The path leads towards this but then turns left (south, sign 'Great Wood') on a path between a wall and a wire fence to reach a stile into the wood itself.

Almost immediately the path forks, a spur leading steeply downhill. Keep left here, climbing very slightly, but then contouring on the level almost below the distinctive white buttresses of Walla Crag high above. Very shortly, the now broad track inclines more noticeably and is soon galloping down-hill to reach the gate outside the car park.

Derwentwater and Skiddaw seen from the top of Cat Gill

46. *Falcon Crag and Ashness Bridge*

Best Map: OS 1:25 000 Outdoor Leisure 4, North Western area

Distance: About 3 miles/4.8km

Highest elevation reached: About 1080ft/329m

Height gained: About 790ft/241m

Star rating: ∗ ∗ ∗

Level of exertion: Quite low

Time for the round: About 2 hours

Terrain: All on good grassy paths.

Outstandingly beautiful landscape is what makes this very short walk such a delight. The combination of fine trees, steep crags, and rushing waters tumbling into the islet-dotted lake, all in close and pleasing proximity, is at its best in this part of Borrowdale. This walk could easily be combined with the previous walk 45, Cat Gill and Walla Crag, but only by omitting Cat Gill, which would be a pity and is why I am keeping it as a separate one.

Start from the National Trust car park in Great Wood (grid ref 272213) about a mile south of Keswick along Borrowdale Road (small parking charge), then go out of the top right-hand corner (south-east) through the gate where there is a sign 'Ashness Bridge and Walla Crag'. The track swings right and then forks; take the right fork, on the level and passing beneath mature larch, beech and oak trees until, on reaching the beck tumbling down Cat Gill, it forks again. (This is exactly the same start as for Walk 45, Cat Gill and Walla Crag.) One path leads up the gill and is for the return, the other leads ahead across a footbridge and then emerges from the trees to disclose a fine view of both Upper and Lower Falcon Crags, as well as a wide vista across Derwentwater to Causey Pike, other Derwent fells and up Borrowdale. Lower Falcon Crag, in particular, is a favourite with rock-climbers, not only because of the quality of the climbing but because of the proximity of the road, since many of them nowadays don't believe in walking any distance to get onto the rock. The modern fashion for lurid-coloured tights makes some of the climbers very conspicuous as you ramble along directly below the crag. The path forks as you do: ignore the right-hand one which leads down to Borrowdale Road, and take the left-hand one which rises gently through bracken, contouring across the fellside above the road to Watendlath and then curving up to a ladder-stile at a wall. From here the path slopes down to Barrow Beck, where the road crosses it at Ashness

Derwentwater and Skiddaw seen from Ashness Bridge

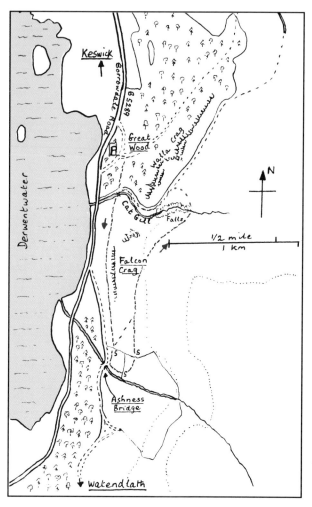

Bridge. This is a particularly well-known viewpoint and walkers and tourists (for a few cars can be parked nearby) feel compelled to stop and admire what is one of the finest outlooks over Derwentwater.

From Ashness Bridge, take the path up the left side of Barrow Beck to a step-stile over the wire fence only fifty paces or so from the bridge, then take the good grassy path climbing back sharp left (north) and making for another and higher ladder-stile over the wall you crossed on the approach to Ashness Bridge. The continuation of this path rises gently across the fellside well above Falcon Crag, allowing more superb views across Derwentwater, and achieves a high point just before reaching the head of Cat Gill.

This is probably the easiest and shortest walk I can think of in the area and when I proposed it to a close relative recently those were the two key words, 'short' and 'easy'. On this path rising up the fell from Ashness Bridge, admittedly the steepest bit of an almost level walk, he stopped about five times. For the first three I thought it was to admire the view. But I then realised, with some concern, that he was checking his heart pace-maker. He made it to where the zig-zag path rising up Cat Gill is clearly visible as you contour round its head to reach it, beside the wall rising from Great Wood. He suffered a few palpitations on the faily steep decent down the gill, and then fell over, giving us a few as well. But he reached Great Wood safely and was soon smiling when a right turn returned him to the car. It just proves that this is a good walk, even for crocks. And he agrees.

47. King's How and the Bowder Stone

Best Map: OS 1:25 000 Outdoor Leisure 4, North Western area

Distance: About 2½ miles/4km

Highest elevation reached: 1286ft/392m

Height gained: About 1120ft/341m

Star rating: * * *

Level of exertion: Medium

Time for the round: About 2½ hours

Terrain: A mixture of good grassy paths, a rocky gully (with good footing) and a fairly steep descent, which should not prove difficult.

This is a wholly delightful walk through some of the finest scenery in beautiful Borrowdale while the modest climb to King's How is still enough to make you feel that you have achieved something worthwhile. The lovely views down Derwentwater would make it worthwhile anyway.

Quayfoot car park (small fee) is just south of Grange, where Borrowdale narrows to its 'jaws' (grid ref 253168). From the upper car park, cross the wire fence by a stile and walk ENE through parkland dotted with birches. A better path is soon joined, leading through some overgrown slate quarries where you may spot the circular entrance to a big cave which formed part of the workings. Rising across more grassy parkland, the path swings east through more silver birches onto a low ridge separating Borrowdale from the almost hidden and enclosed valley of Troutdale, giving a good view of the splendid Greatend Crag. Pass through a gate but then, before reaching a ladder-stile where the path leads down into Trout-dale, turn right (south) and start to climb a stonier path rising through the woods. This path rapidly improves, having been virtually reconstructed in recent years to form a rock staircase up a shallow gully beneath the trees.

You emerge onto a shoulder and all around is a wonderfully knobbly skyline with birch trees scattered among the heather. The main path continues easily but then rises again to the wide, level, boggy area of Long Moss. The path to the height of King's How rises from its northern end, marked by a fine yew tree, up a grassy runnel onto another shoulder from where there is a view down the length of Borrowdale. A very short, easy rock scramble leads to a better viewpoint, improving ever more as you gain height. On the way, you pass a slate plaque inscribed (in part) 'Raised in loving memory of King Edward VII, Grange Fell is

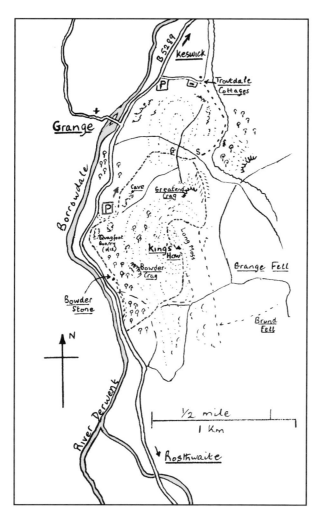

dedicated by his sister Louise as a sanctuary of rest and peace.' On the whole it still is just that and the top is a fantastic viewpoint.

Descend to the south (there are several paths), towards the hamlet of Rosthwaite further up Borrowdale, to reach a solid stone wall which can be seen ahead. Turn downhill alongside this and the path leads steeply through more lovely woodland of birch and yew to reach the Borrowdale Road at a gate. Here turn right on the roadside path and in about three hundred paces reach another gate and stile with a sign 'Footpath to Bowder Stone'. A stony track quickly leads to this curiosity; it is quite unmistakable with its ladder of 28 or 29 steps – although we counted we could not agree on the final number.

Considering its bulk, the Bowder Stone rests upon a very tiny base and, like the Leaning Tower of Pisa, could well fall over. In the late eighteenth century a banker named Pocklington, after whom Pocklington's Isle in Derwentwater is named, had a little hole cut through the base so that an old lady, specially hired for the purpose, could lie down and shake hands through the gap with any tourist brave enough to lie on the far side and risk being crushed if it collapsed. So far it has not done so.

The broad track continues past the old Quayfoot Quarry to reach the road at the precise point where you turn uphill again to the car park and, you hope, the ice-cream van.

Descent to Borrowdale from King's How

48. Tarn at Leaves and Bessyboot from Borrowdale

Best Map: OS 1:25 000 Outdoor Leisure 4, North
    Western area

Distance: About 6 miles/9.6km

Highest elevation reached: 1807ft/551m

Height gained: About 1450ft/442m

Star rating: * *

Level of exertion: Fairly high

Time for the round: About 3 hours

Terrain: The grassy or stony fell paths are not
    particularly clear above valley level but
    natural features enable straightforward route-
    finding.

The Borrowdale Fells between Grains Gill and
Langstrath contain some of the wildest, most
crumpled and knobbly landscape in the Lake District.
This short walk climbs to a treeless tarn high on the
broad ridge, visits a rocky tor overlooking it and then
finds a way down the far side to link up with the path
down Lakeland's longest and only 'strath'.

There is a large car park at Seatoller at the head of
Borrowdale (grid ref 245137) or you can park on the
side of the road nearer Strands Bridge. Just east of
Strands Bridge is a gate and a signed footpath leads
across fields from here to cross the beck from Combe
Gill by an old stone packhorse bridge. From here
there is at present no sign on the ground of the path
which the OS map shows as rising directly up the
slope to the south-east (facing you as soon as you have
crossed the bridge) before it swings south-west to
contour the fellside higher up. There is, however, a
good path heading to the right (south) along the
bank, which soon reaches an old building, now
restored and half-hidden in trees beside the river and
which, a sign reads, was evidently a former corn mill
for the valley. Round the back can be seen an old iron
water-wheel and the leat that diverted water from the
beck. A little further upstream is a small water
authority building, then the path becomes boggy as it
passes a little weir, then twin waterfalls. Appreciably
drier ground now leads to a gateway in the intake wall
and the faint path climbs a stony slope beside the beck
in a shallow gill.

Occasionally cairns mark the way as you cross the
head of the gill and climb a grassy tongue which leads
beside the much deeper ravine of Rottenstone Gill,
emerging onto a boggy area where it fades into the

*Looking towards
Bessyboot and
Rosthwaite Cam from
near Seatoller*

171

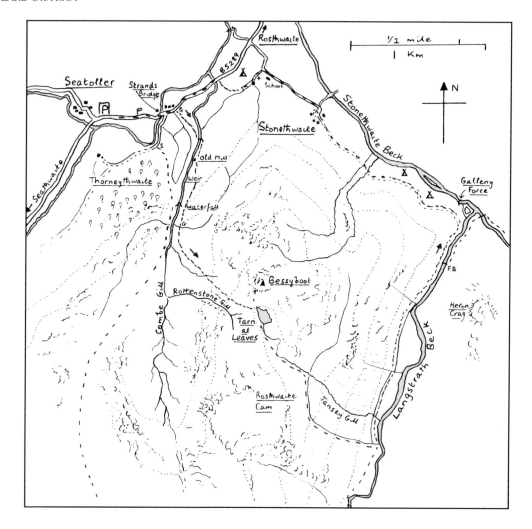

fellside. Just a little further and over a slight rise Tarn at Leaves appears, partly hidden behind a rocky spur and almost surrounded by heather and bracken-covered humps of knobbly rock. There is not a tree in sight, but that is hardly surprising, given both the altitude and the sheep roaming the fells.

A faint path leads from the north end of the tarn up to the cairn on the most prominent of the nearby rocky humps; this is Bessyboot. A superb panoramic view is visible from here: High Raise, the Langdale Pikes, Glaramara, Great Gable and Pillar, High Stile, Catbells, Skiddaw, Blencathra and most of the Dodds' ridge. It is one to savour before returning to the tarn.

Unless you return to Borrowdale by the way of ascent, the way to go now is south-east, down the line of Tansey Gill draining into Langstrath Beck. At the intake wall, just trend rightwards and down the brackeny slopes beside it to reach the well-used path in the valley bottom. This leads gently down the lovely Langstrath with its delightful river pools and then, past the popular camping fields, to the hamlet of Stonethwaite. Following the metalled track from here, a turn off left, just past the school and signed 'Borrowdale Road via Chapel Farm', leads through the farm yard and a sheep pen. When I went through it was packed with sheep and I had to do some energetic dodging to avoid a smelly doom. Good paths beyond lead to Borrowdale Road and a left turn gets you to the car.

The old water-wheel and corn mill, Combe Gill Beck

49. High Spy from Grange

Best Map: OS 1:25 000 Outdoor Leisure 4, North Western area

Distance: About 5½ miles/8.8km

Highest elevation reached: 2142ft/653m

Height gained: About 1820ft/555m

Star rating: * *

Level of exertion: Fairly high

Time for the round: About 4 hours

Terrain: Good paths generally, although they are not very clear for a short way on High Spy and on part of the descent.

This walk follows a path through lovely woods beside the River Derwent, climbs past old slate quarries to the high fells overlooking Newlands, then makes a dramatic return to Borrowdale, using a narrow but perfectly safe path below steep crags and improbably steep fellside.

Park somewhere in Grange; it is not usually too difficult. Now take the metalled track opposite one of the two churches and signed 'Public Bridleway Honister Rosthwaite Seatoller' (grid ref 253175). When it turns right for Hollows Farm, continue straight ahead on a rough walled track beneath trees beside the camping fields. Reaching the wide bend of the River Derwent at Gowder Dub, the track forks at a finger-post. The right-hand path leads beside a smaller beck, shortly crosses to the other side and then, beyond a gate and outside the woods, rises up Broadslack Gill, overlooked by the high cliffs of Castle Crag on the left and the much higher ones of Goat Crag on the right.

Reaching a col, with fine views of the head of Borrowdale, continue along the broad terrace for a short way but then trend rightwards to the foot of Tongue Gill. Paths go up both sides of the gill, obviously washed away by flood water from time to time, but then old slate spoil-tips come into view ahead on the left and you can make use of the old grassy incline rising to the long-closed Rigghead Quarries. Here, at this level, you will find a derelict building, some old rails leading into a tunnel and a large cave, from which water will drip down your neck if you enter. Beyond this the slope leads up to a stile and to a still-standing building marked on the map as a 'climbing-hut', although it doesn't look much used. The ancient pulley is completely rusted and immovable, but a workman using it would have had a good view down to the fields of Borrowdale far below.

From here an easy path slants across slate spoil and

View to Glaramara and the Scafells from the top of High Spy

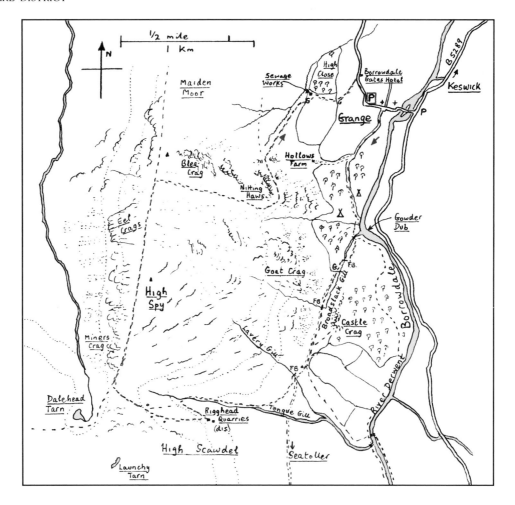

just below several more large spoil tips to rejoin the path rising up the gill, which now continues past the entrances to several more levels. Above these a cairned path leads to a stile and so to the head of the gill at a depression on the broad-backed High Spy ridge.

The path fades here but grassy slopes to the north lead towards the highest land, and the substantial cairn on High Spy is soon reached. From here a well-used path leads along the crest of the ridge above Eel Crags, then dips to a shallow depression before rising again to another rocky eminence crowned by an obvious cairn (Blea Crag). About 300 yds/90m *before* reaching it, turn off to the east down the depression. There is little sign of the path (despite it being part of the Cumbria Way) until you have descended easy grass slopes, but then it is cairned into a wide heathery depression behind three rock humps. Increasingly obvious now, it snakes behind these humps to reach a little col and then, in a quite exciting situation for a path, passes beneath a rocky buttress (marked as Nitting Haws on the map) to reach a second grassy and less obvious col. From here, ignore the path continuing beyond across the fellside and instead turn downhill, north-east, just right of a developing beck to reach a gate beside the tiny sewage works. The signed path now leads back to the road opposite the Borrowdale Gates Hotel, just outside Grange.

In Broadslack Gill, looking to Skiddaw

50. Barrow and Newlands Beck from Braithwaite

> **Best Map:** OS 1:25 000 Outdoor Leisure 4, North Western area
>
> **Distance:** About 5¼ miles/8.5km
>
> **Highest elevation reached:** 1493ft/455m
>
> **Height gained:** About 1200ft/366m
>
> **Star rating:** */**
>
> **Level of exertion:** Medium
>
> **Time for the round:** About 3 hours
>
> **Terrain:** Good paths and tracks

A pleasant climb up a grassy ridge, an optional visit to a well-loved pub near the half way point (much appreciated on a day of indifferent weather) and an easy ramble along the Newlands Beck for the return are the chief ingredients of this most attractive walk.

Park somewhere in Braithwaite, the little village west of Keswick at the foot of Whinlatter, then start the walk from the point where the drive up to Braithwaite Lodge (farm) leaves the Buttermere road (grid ref 232235). If you are lucky, there is room for about two cars here. Walk up the drive, and then through two gates ('Bridleway' sign) just right of the farm and up a grassy slope beyond to a signpost marked 'Barrow' and 'Newlands'. A soft-option route, the one signed 'Newlands', takes a lower grassy path which avoids climbing Barrow entirely, skirts round to the left above a little conifer wood and rejoins the road further on, but we know that any indulgence such as a visit to a pub must be earned by a little hard work first.

So the best way is to follow the line of pigeon-hole steps that lead, fairly steeply at first, up the grassy ridge ahead. The angle soon eases, slightly. A glow of health, or something anyway, should be felt as we press on with heart pounding and legs trembling, to collapse on the little pile of stones on the summit of Barrow.

That's the hard work over; almost everything else is either downhill or on the level. Take time to admire the views to Causey Pike and Sail, to Grisedale Pike and Crag Hill, before continuing along the ridge to where an obvious path runs off to the south-east down Stonycroft Gill.

This path descends quite rapidly and soon reaches the unfenced metalled road which is followed briefly northwards before turning off to the right down the

Skiddaw seen from the bank of Newlands Beck near Farm Uzzicar

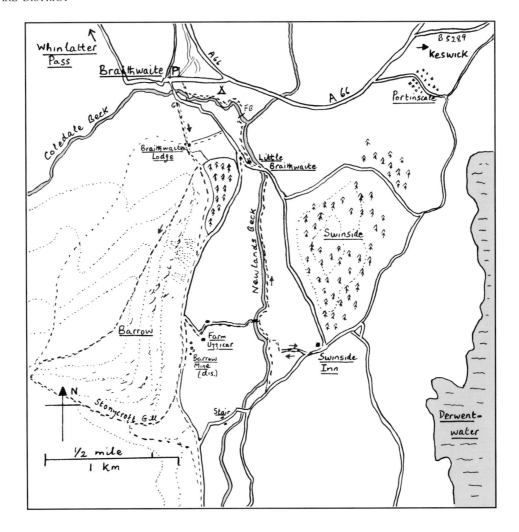

track towards the buildings of Farm Uzzicar, by-passing several spoil-heaps next to the former gold mines. Turn left in front of Farm Uzzicar and follow the track past the adjacent Low Uzzicar, continuing along a fenced and hedged lane winding pleasantly across fields to reach the Newlands Beck at a hump-backed stone bridge.

To reach the Swinside Inn, this is the point at which you turn right (south) along the bank to reach another short lane which itself leads to the road just a hundred paces from the pub. Return to the bridge the same way, then continue north along the grassy embankment above the river which is here quite wide, enjoying very easy walking with good views, towards Skiddaw in particular.

Temporarily leave the riverside path at Little Braithwaite, crossing the road bridge to walk into the hamlet but turning off the road in only fifty paces or so to pass behind a barn to where two wicket gates lead back to the beck again. There is a gate a short distance ahead but don't go through it and upset the sheep usually grazing there. Instead, keep alongside the stream as it curves right (north-east) but then turn left along the bank of Coledale Beck at its confluence with Newlands Beck. Cross to the far bank by a little footbridge, beyond which the path takes you into the large caravan and camping-site. Keep close to the beck here and the path skirts the edge of the site and joins the road in Braithwaite to complete the round.

Swinside Inn from Farm Uzzicar, Walla Crag on the skyline

51. Barf and Lord's Seat

Best Map: OS 1:25 000 Outdoor Leisure 4, North Western area

Distance: About 3½ miles/5.6km

Highest elevation reached: 1811ft/552m

Height gained: About 1500ft/457m

Star rating: */**

Level of exertion: Medium/high

Time for the round: About 2½ hours

Terrain: Approach is up a fairly steep path through woods, so it can remain wet underfoot after rain. Good grassy paths/tracks otherwise.

Travellers along the A66 road from Keswick to Cockermouth can hardly fail to spot a white-painted rock looking like a chess piece on the steep fellside above the Swan Hotel at Thornthwaite, near the south end of Bassenthwaite Lake. This is The Bishop. Above his ecclesiastical head, broken rocks rise to Barf. A little higher in the firmament, but easily reached, is Lord's Seat. For the fairly fit, or those who aspire to be so, this walk will be well worth the effort; others may find a stroll around the perimeter of Powterhow Wood to be a pleasant alternative, and they will find a signed footpath to follow with minimum exertion.

There is a good car park at Powter How, next to the Swan Hotel (grid ref 222265) and opposite it a finger-post points up a metalled track, which joins the drive to Beckstones. Only fifty paces beyond the junction, turn right through a gate and up a grassy path through woods at the base of a scree slope. At the top of the slope is The Bishop; at the bottom, as befits his lowlier station, is a much smaller rock, also painted white, called The Clerk. There isn't much enjoyment in scrabbling up the scree slope to inspect The Bishop. I can tell you here that it is a solid lump of rock about 8ft/2.4m high. The story of this stone is most fascinating. In 1783 the then Bishop of Londonderry stayed at The Swan on his way home to Northern Ireland and made a bet, in his cups no doubt, that he could ride his pack-pony as far as Lord's Seat. He only got as far as this rock when his pony stumbled, fell and both horse and rider were killed. They were buried together at the point now marked by The Clerk, at the foot of the slope, and the stone was painted white by order of the landlord. The painting is renewed annually: the fee for the work used to be 'five shillings and a quart of ale'; nowadays this is 'negotiable'.

Barf seen from Lord's Seat, with Skiddaw beyond

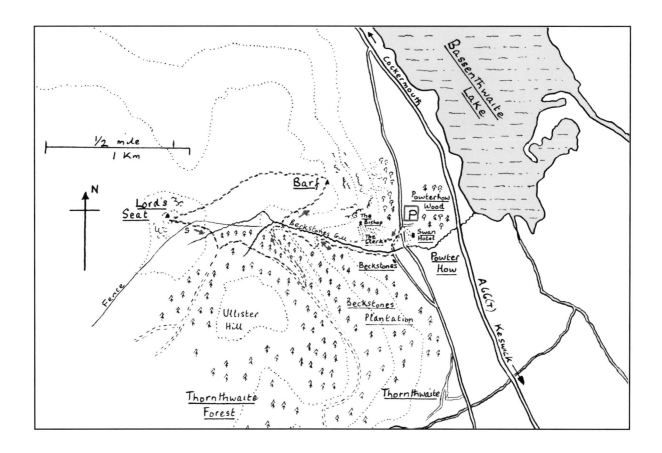

The path skirts below scree beside Beckstones Gill, fords the beck and rises up the side of the gill, marked by Forestry Commission posts. At one point, the path scrambles up a short rocky staircase, then up a wide zigzag beneath the trees, briefly joins a Forestry track and then turns off it to a stile over a wire fence at the head of the gill. Leave the forest here, cross the stream and swing northwards up bilberry slopes to reach a little cairn and scattered rocks on Barf. The views along Bassenthwaite are no less than you might expect. From Barf, a path leads due west across the upper reaches of a depression, then grass slopes, and finally to Lord's Seat, adorned by two iron fence posts.

Just down the slope to the east is a stile at a wire fence and the Forestry path from here soon reaches a junction, where it is important to turn sharp left (north-east). This path soon joins a broad Forestry track contouring across the fellside to the south-east, but do not walk too far along it admiring views over Keswick as you must turn back sharp left on another track joining it; there's a post with the number 7 on it at this junction. This track, soon becoming grassy, leads back towards Beckstones Gill, takes a sharp right turn (post number 22 on the junction) and joins the section of Forestry track used on the ascent, near the stile. You may now reverse the ascent route, but don't forget to turn left off this Forestry track in about a hundred paces to pick up the path through the trees again.

The Bishop on the slopes of Barf

52. Knott Rigg and Sail Beck from Newlands Hause

> **Best Map:** OS 1:25 000 Outdoor Leisure 4, North Western area
>
> **Distance:** About 4 miles/6.4km
>
> **Highest elevation reached:** 1824ft/556m
>
> **Height gained:** About 1230ft/375m
>
> **Star rating:** * *
>
> **Level of exertion:** Medium
>
> **Time for the round:** About 2½ hours
>
> **Terrain:** Grassy paths; generally firm underfoot apart from a boggy col and a stream crossing (just pick the right stones on which to cross . . .)

A dramatic defile, seen by motorists as they climb from Buttermere to Newlands Hause, forms another pass between the Buttermere Valley and that of the Newlands Beck. The Buttermere side of this defile is drained by Sail Beck, with steep slopes rising on the one hand to the impressive heights of Crag Hill and Sail and, on the other, to the much lower ridge of Knott Rigg and Ard Crags. Incidentally Wainwright is very emphatic that the OS name of

'Crag Hill' for the highest point was and is incorrect and that the local usage for a century and more was for the whole fell to be called Eel Crag. So, for walkers of a generation even older than mine who think I'm writing rubbish when I use 'Crag Hill' when what I really mean is 'Eel Crag' (despite the OS) I can only apologise. This walk doesn't go up it anyway, whatever is its proper name. We go over the Knott Rigg ridge and experience some of this grand country the easy way, particularly since the start is from a height of 1092ft/333m. The sting in the tail is that the walk ends with a 500ft/152m ascent – but it's worth it.

Start from the car park at Newlands Hause (grid ref 193176), the highest point on the road which runs between Buttermere and Braithwaite, west of Keswick. The path climbing to the north from here towards Knott Rigg ('Public footpath' sign) is over close-cropped grass and not very clear, but as the ridge sharpens it goes more obviously up a line of pigeon-hole steps and a few rockier places and soon attains the handful of stones which make up the 'cairn' on top of Knott Rigg. Just beyond it, the ground drops steeply down the secret little ravine of Ill Gill, where an ancient oak wood clings to the fellside. Further east, one's eye can travel over a line of no fewer than seven ridges, the furthest being that of the Dodds and Helvellyn.

Knott Rigg, on the right, from the Newlands Hause road

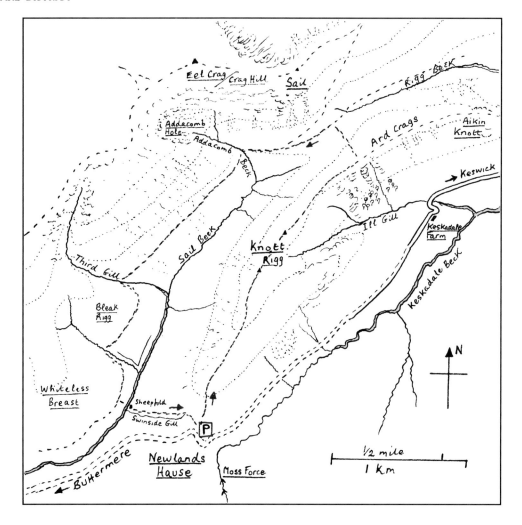

The path along the ridge-top undulates a little now, opposite but much lower than the dark combe which was gouged by ice out of the scarp edge of Crag Hill and known as Addacomb Hole. The path then rises just a little to Ard Crags, whose rocks overlook Keskadale Farm, a long way below. Looking down easy grass slopes from here to the north-west, to the path crossing the Sail Pass, it is clear that this is quite close and easily attainable, so that is the way to go now.

The pass is soon reached; it's boggy, like many are, but you are soon on the excellent, firm path that leads through the pass and can turn left (south-west) along it. It keeps quite high above the line of the Sail Beck, but below the heather-clad slopes and with a grand view of Sail Beck, like a ribbon winding below the crinkled gills on the flank of Knott Rigg. After crossing the Addacomb Beck the traverse continues, crossing Third Gill and then the flank of Bleak Rigg as far as the next, un-named gill. On its other side, the path now turns noticeably downhill and there is, sadly, nothing for it but to lose height. When opposite a little sheepfold beside Swinside Gill, which drains land directly below Newlands Hause, the time has come to cross Sail Beck (normally very easy) and climb back up sheep tracks through the bracken slopes to the car park. If you set out on this walk at the beginning of, or just after a great deluge of heavy rain and cannot cross the beck, you'll have to walk down to the bridge in Buttermere and then thumb a lift back up the road.

Looking north up Sail Beck, with Knott Rigg on the right

189

53. Brackenthwaite Hows and Lanthwaite Wood

Best Map: OS 1:25 000 Outdoor Leisure 4, North Western area

Distance: About 3 miles/4.8km

Highest elevation reached: About 656ft/200m

Height gained: About 663ft/202m

Star rating: **/***

Level of exertion: Low

Time for the round: About 2 hours

Terrain: Mostly on good grassy or firm paths.

This short, low-level and very good all-weather walk has much more variety than a glance at the map would suggest, as it progresses over undulating land and finishes with a pleasant stroll through Lanthwaite Wood.

Park at Lanthwaite Green Farm at the northern end of Crummock Water (grid ref 158207). Take the path from here towards the deep defile of Gasgale Gill, between Grasmoor and Whiteside, but before reaching the foot of the gorge, veer leftwards (northeast) so that you can cross the Liza Beck emerging from it by a footbridge. Continue up a short slope towards the top corner of the intake wall ahead, where it curves to the left (north) and contours across the fellside below the steep slopes of Whiteside End. A good grassy path will be found shadowing this intake wall, with green enclosed pastures on its other side and beyond them, over Crummock Water, can now be seen Mellbreak and the fells north of Loweswater, Low Fell and Darling Fell.

Reaching a high ladder-stile over the wall, cross and go down a sloping and sometimes boggy field to reach a little beck crossed on stones. A little further on, the Liza Beck is crossed again, this time by a footbridge which reaches the road at a gate next to Beck House. The path beyond the gate opposite (sign 'Footpath to Scale Hill') leads towards the farm at Pickett Howe, but its owners have provided a better route for our walk than the path shown on the OS map. This new route is marked 'permissive path' on a couple of gates and leads across pasture land to the south-west, gently slanting across the slopes of Brackenthwaite Hows towards the top edge of a wood, mostly of conifers, and so onto a grassy crest overlooking Crummock Water, with the highest point of Brackenthwaite Hows being just a little higher and further away, to the south-east.

Turn right (west) here along this crest to a stile into an oak wood, which also has some unusual multi-

Crummock Water from the edge of Lanthwaite Wood

191

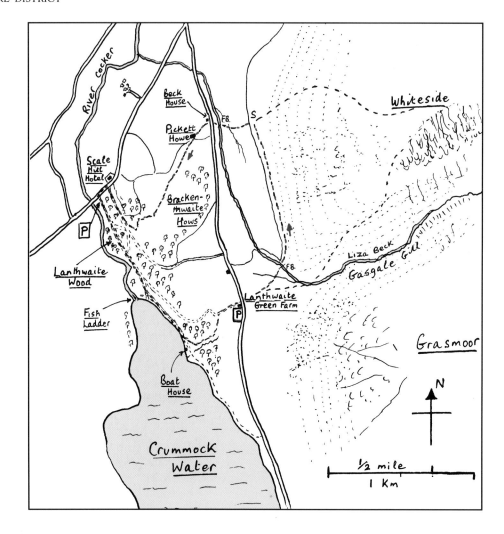

trunked pine trees. The path initially goes down gently but then more steeply, swinging left and then descending in zigzags down some made steps at the steepest places. When you intersect with a broad track, turn right and you will quickly emerge from the trees on the road almost opposite the Scale Hill Hotel. A left turn here takes you down the road a short way to another left turn where a track leads back into Lanthwaite Wood again, passing immediately above the car park and continuing south-east.

There are several confusing tracks as you walk through this fine mixed wood and your long range visibility is restricted at this stage but if you bear right each time the track forks you will be led to the edge of Crummock Water at its northern end and all will be clear once more. Here you may inspect the 'fish-ladder' which enables fish to swim up into the lake and by-pass the weir and you may cross the two footbridges across the double outflows from the lake to take a stroll along the west bank.

Back on the east bank, continue on a track very close to the shore, allowing views across the lake. Then, immediately before reaching the boat house ahead, turn left onto a slighter path which rises through the trees and then alongside a little beck. At a wall enclosing the wood, it swings left (north-west) and joins a major track leading to a gate at the edge of the wood. Cross an open field, looking directly up Gasgale Gill again, and gates and stiles lead easily to a grassy drive at the side of Lanthwaite Green Farm and back to the car.

Crummock Water, near the fish-ladder

193

54. Darling Fell and Low Fell, Loweswater

> **Best Map:** OS 1:25 000 Outdoor Leisure 4, North Western area
>
> **Distance:** About 5½ miles/8.8km
>
> **Highest elevation reached:** 1352ft/412m
>
> **Height gained:** About 1245ft/379m
>
> **Star rating:** **/***
>
> **Level of exertion:** Medium
>
> **Time for the round:** About 3 hours
>
> **Terrain:** On fairly vague paths on the grassy fell tops, with a steep descent from Low Fell that may jar geriatric knees; otherwise on good tracks and paths.

Superb views, particularly over Crummock Water and to Grasmoor and Mellbreak, are the highlights of this splendid walk over the low fells to the north of Loweswater.

The best place to park is just north of Loweswater, by the phone box opposite a metalled track signed 'Bridleway Mossergate' (grid ref 118225). Walk up this track, turning north up a much rougher one (signed 'Path to Mosser Fell') which rises to a gate at another metalled track. Turn sharp right here (southeast) with views over Loweswater, until this track starts to descend, shortly reaching a stile and footpath on the left, signed for Foulsyke, leading onto more open fell.

The OS map suggests that the route ahead is up the steepest slope and then through a band of crags, but sensible walkers have had more care for their persons than to do that and chosen the easiest line which shows as a faint path rising up grassy slopes alongside the wire fence. It then curves rightwards beside old fence posts up a grassy ridge to a stile at another fence, reaching the cairn on Darling Fell just beyond it. It can now be seen that the unusually precise parcelling of the land on these fell-tops is more obtrusive on the map than on the ground, for the walls have mostly gone and wire fences have taken their place. It is, however, the prospect to the south-west that commands the attention, with a marvellous view along Crummock Water.

An unexpectedly steep descent beyond Darling Fell, shadowing the line of the fence to the east, leads to a crossing of Crabtree Beck after which the faint path turns uphill again, with the fence on the left, to a stile on a little col. Turning right (south) here, a

View to Buttermere, Crummock Water and Mellbreak from Darling Fell

195

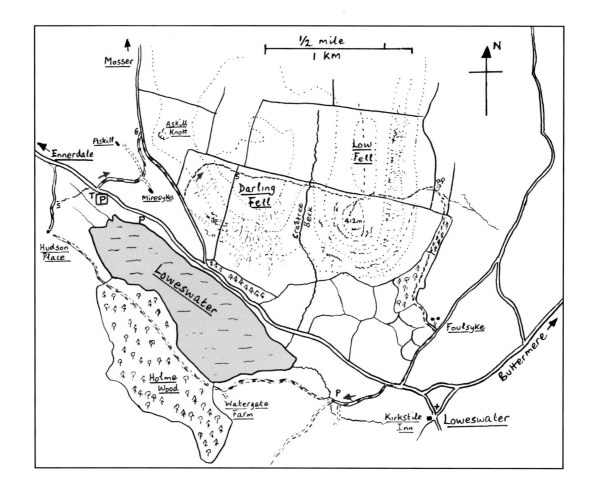

short climb leads to a large cairn on Low Fell (spot-height 412m) from where the views are even wider ranging, with Whiteside and Grasmoor now included in the view as well as Mellbreak and Crummock Water. The OS rather perversely only give the name Low Fell to a shoulder to the north of this fine viewpoint marked by such an obvious cairn.

Returning to the col there is a grass path heading north but no sign of one leaving Low Fell to the east so descend steeply with care beside the wire fence, heading for the base of the fell where a fence and wall meet by a little group of trees. An old stile at a gap here leads to a recognisable path down a little gill, turning south beside a fence, then passing through a conifer plantation and along the lower edge of more woods, curving round to reach Foulsyke. Turning south-west, the metalled road from here leads to a T-junction; a left and then a right turn here will quickly take you to the especially welcoming Kirkstile Inn which will send you on your way with a happy glow.

Otherwise, turn right at the road signed for Ennerdale and Mockerkin and then left down a metalled bridleway. The tarmac ends at a little car park and then the right fork on the broad track ahead leads along the obvious path through Holme Wood beside the lovely Loweswater, continuing to Hudson Place Farm. Turning right and downhill here, a stile and footpath soon leads across the fields to the start.

Grasmoor and Crummock Water seen from Low Fell

55. Whitewater Dash and Great Calva

Best Maps: OS 1:25 000 Pathfinder 576 Caldbeck;
OS 1:50 000 Landranger 90 Penrith, Keswick
& Ambleside area

Distance: About 6 miles/9.6km

Highest elevation reached: 2264ft/690m

Height gained: About 1562ft/476m

Star rating: */**

General level of exertion: Medium

Time for the round: About 3–3½ hours

Terrain: Firm tracks for about 4½ miles/7.2km;
rough fell paths over heather and grass for the
remainder.

Almost in the middle of the (virtually treeless) Skiddaw Forest is Great Calva. Seen from the A591 east of Keswick, a tantalising glimpse of its apparently conical top may often be seen along the deep trench of the Glenderaterra Beck separating Skiddaw from Blencathra, but it looks remote and inaccessible. In fact, there is a fast and easy approach, also used by the Cumbria Way and passing by the waterfalls of the Whitewater Dash. Walkers are specifically requested by the National Park to avoid Great Calva during the months from the beginning of April until the end of June because a number of protected bird species nest there. Dogs must be under close control for the same reason. This should be no hardship as the best time for walking on these fells is autumn and winter anyway.

Parking for cars is very limited along the narrow road leading off the A591 at the side of Bassenthwaite Lake (the only 'lake' in the Lake District) which is signed for 'Orthwaite', but a few places can be found at the end of the metalled public bridleway just south of Peter House Farm (grid ref 249323, signed 'Skiddaw House and Threlkeld via Dash Falls'). Follow this until the turn off to Dash Farm – so sited that it is not in the permanent shadow that afflicts Dead Crags; then leave it for the unmetalled track continuing up the valley. The cairn on Little Calva soon comes into view ahead and the track curves across a depression on the fellside below Dead Crags to reach a point at the top of the waterfalls of the Whitewater Dash, now seen to be a series of falls rather than one single one. The track crosses the Dash Beck by a stony bridge which is fifty paces beyond a gate and stile at the top of the falls.

The Uldale Fells seen from the path to Whitewater Dash

199

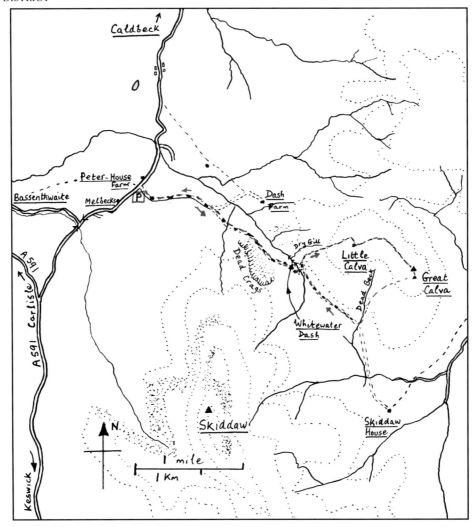

Leave it immediately beyond the bridge and make for a faint path climbing fairly steeply through heather to the north-east, beside a wire fence and up the edge of a shallow gill (Dry Gill). The steep pull soon eases and then a shallow grassy groove enables more height to be gained, shadowing the line of the fence and finally trending right (south) to the prominent cairn on Little Calva. The view from here isn't the best one of Skiddaw, which is from the south, but it is an impressive one nevertheless.

Great Calva is to the east, not looking conical at all from here, and the easiest way there follows the line of the fence-posts to a cairn on a rounded hump of land, then curves round the head of the boggy depression drained lower down by Dead Beck. A last short rise leads to a large cairn and a partially roofed tiny stone shelter, with two more cairns and another windbreak nearby. Excluding the views to the backs of Skiddaw and Blencathra, the best one is to the south, where a glimpse of Thirlmere can be seen along St John's in the Vale, but the sense of being miles from anywhere is quite profound.

For the descent, a path can be seen heading downhill through heather to the south-west, towards Skiddaw, tracing the course of Dead Beck to the little bridge where the bridleway to Skiddaw House crosses it. Turn right (north-west) here and the good track soon leads you back to the top of the Whitewater Dash and the outward route.

Dash Farm and White Hause behind

201

56. Great Sca Fell

> *Best Maps:* OS 1:25 000 Pathfinder 576 Caldbeck;
> OS 1:50 000 Landranger 90 Penrith, Keswick
> & Ambleside area
>
> *Distance:* About 6¼ miles/10km
>
> *Highest elevation reached:* 2136ft/651m
>
> *Height gained:* About 1316ft/401m
>
> *Star rating:* */* *
>
> *Level of exertion:* Medium
>
> *Time for the round:* About 4 hours
>
> *Terrain:* A mixture of firm and grassy tracks with
> faint paths over the grassy moorland. Not
> suitable for misty weather.

Great Sca Fell has nothing to do with Scafell or Scafell Pike. It is just inside the Lake District National Park boundary in the Uldale Fells, north of Great Calva, at the 'back o'Skidda'. All the fells here have more in common with the Howgills than the rugged mountains beyond the jaws of Borrowdale; they are grassy, rounded, have few fences and fewer walls and give undramatic but very pleasant walking.

The best approach for this walk is from Greenhead, reached by driving from the north end of Bassenthwaite Lake on the narrow road to Uldale and then on towards Caldbeck. Just after joining the unfenced B5299, turn right along another unfenced road to Greenhead, where there is parking for numerous cars on the unfenced verge of the road (grid ref 287371).

From here, head south-west along a track, metalled as far as a turn-off, then unmetalled and stony, going over a slight rise to ford the beck flowing down Charleton Gill. Just beyond the ford and almost round the bend, turn left (south-east) up a grassy path. This is rather vague initially but soon becomes very obvious, leading along a gently rising ledge up the flank of the deeply cut Charleton Gill. At its head, the gill fades into several shallow watercourses and the path curves round the top of them heading towards an obvious tall cairn on high land ahead but then by-passing it. Leaving the path, a short grassy slope leads to it, with its adjacent windbreak, but this is Little Sca Fell. Great Sca Fell, only slightly higher and marked by an insignificant cairn is about 400 paces south, across a little depression. Returning to the cairn on Little Sca Fell, another one is visible almost due north on Brae Fell which is obviously visited as a narrow grassy path leads to its little stone

Looking north-east down Ramps Gill from Brae Fell

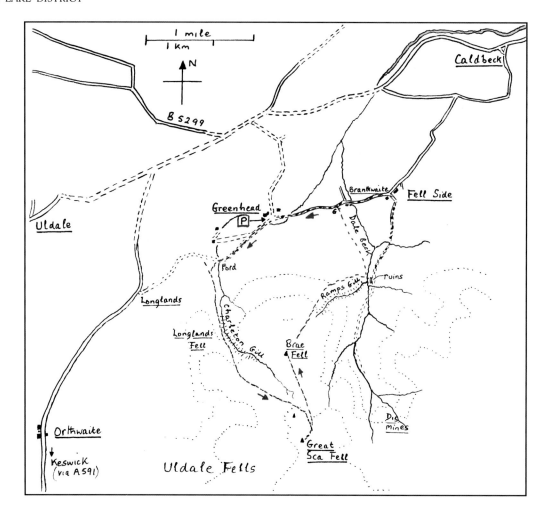

windbreak, allowing fine views back to the south towards Skiddaw and west to Binsey, seen beyond Over Water.

To the north-east, the grassy slope declines gently towards what increasingly looks like a 'hush', the deep defiles gouged by water out of the flanks of the fells of Swaledale and elsewhere to reveal the lead ore-bearing rocks. It is soon seen to be more a spectacular deep ravine in whose rushy depths a tiny stream rises and drains to join the Dale Beck. This is Ramps Gill and its edge leads to a place where you can easily ford Dale Beck and climb the short slope beyond, passing some very tumbledown but extensive ruined buildings which must have had connections with the former mines in Roughton Gill higher up the valley. A good track is now joined and it leads swiftly to the hamlet of Fell Side, although at its end it is rather galling to be able to see the car and yet be walking further away from it. Fortunately the by-road from Fell Side is extremely quiet, the little hamlet of Branthwaite is soon passed and the car quickly rejoined at Greenhead.

If water in Dale Beck is found to be too deep to ford easily or if you just prefer a shorter but rougher way home, walkers can continue along the west bank, keeping outside the intake walls, and will find a fell-gate, installed by the National Park, leading to the road just west of Branthwaite.

View from Great Sca Fell to Over Water and Binsey

57.   Bowscale Fell and Tarn from Mungrisdale

<table>
<tr><td>

Best Maps: At 1:25 000 scale, both Outdoor Leisure 5, North Eastern area and OS Pathfinder 576 Caldbeck are needed. The walk is all on OS 1:50 000 Landranger 90 Penrith, Keswick & Ambleside area

Distance: About 5½ miles/8.8km

Highest elevation reached: 2303ft/702m

Height gained: About 1530ft/466m

Star rating: *

Level of exertion: Medium

Time for the round: About 3 hours

Terrain: Good grassy or firm tracks on all except the highest land. Not suitable for misty weather.

</td></tr>
</table>

The open rolling northern fells of Lakeland generally offer peaceful and easy walking with few surprises, but the first sight of Bowscale Tarn from above can give a real frisson of pleasure and turn a simple walk into something much more exciting, which is why I have included it.

The start is in the little village of Mungrisdale, just north of the A66 trunk road east of Keswick, where there is parking space opposite the Mill Inn, or round the corner by the phone box (grid ref 362304), just as for Walk 58. From the phone box, a short walled lane, signed for Mungrisdale Common, leads west onto an unfenced track beside the River Glenderamackin. There is a footbridge at the point where the Bullfell Beck joins the river and immediately beyond the bridge the track forks; the better one is the one needed and leads to the right (south-west) into Bannerdale. Once it has curved round a bend, this grassy levelled track leads into the combe of Bannerdale towards the site of former lead mines but take the footpath leaving it to the right; it rises across the grassy flank of The Tongue to reach the northern end of the cirque of Bannerdale Crags.

As soon as the rising path reaches the level one leading leftwards round the cirque, you must turn right, to the north, rising up easy grass slopes with little apparent objective in sight apart from two small cairns. The highest point on this swelling moor, the top of Bowscales Fell, is soon reached, distinguished only by a circular stone windbreak and a little cairn.

There is no sign whatsoever of any lake or tarn from the summit, but a surprise is in store. About fifty paces to the north is another cairn and beyond it a faint path leads to a subsidiary top then continues down the

Lookng south-west along the Glenderamackin River

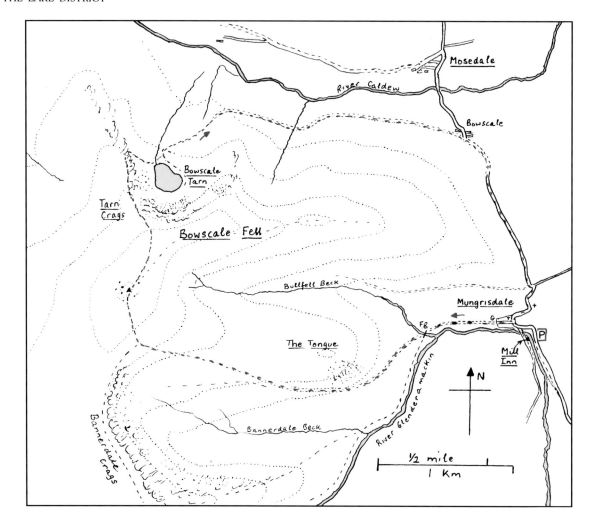

east ridge. You will naturally head towards this, for humans are like sheep, but only go along it for a hundred paces or so before veering off left (north-east from the summit.) You will then be in a most dramatic situation, on the rim of unsuspected steep slopes and broken vegetated ribs of rock high above Bowscale Tarn which glints on a rocky shelf in a deep, glaciated combe below. It is a memorable moment. The tarn itself, like one in Snowdonia which is reputed to contain monocular (one-eyed) fish, is supposed to contain two fish which are thousands of years old. It is a romantic notion suited to the setting. The encircling arm of the combe to the north, beyond which can be seen the slopes of Carrock Fell, is a long, grass-topped ridge, with steep rocky slopes only on the side dropping to the tarn. It looks improbable that a way could lead down them, but that is where it goes. A faint path leads easily along the grassy ridge to a point just before it turns fairly sharply downhill towards the River Caldew and then the path will be seen making a sharp but fairly easy descent heading directly for the outlet from the tarn. When I first came here, coming up from the tarn instead of descending to it, there was hardly any trace of a path at all.

From here a good track slants easily across the northern slope of Bowscale Fell above the River Caldew, to the hamlet of Bowscale, leaving a twenty-minute walk back down the quiet road to Mungrisdale.

Bowscale Tarn from Bowscale Fell

58. Scales Tarn and Souther Fell from Mungrisdale

Best Maps: At 1:25 000 scale, both Outdoor Leisure 5, North Eastern area, and OS Pathfinder 576 Caldbeck are needed. The walk is all on OS 1:50 000 Landranger 90 Penrith, Keswick & Ambleside area

Distance: About 6½ miles/10.4km

Highest elevation reached: About 1936ft/590m

Height gained: About 1470ft/448m

Star rating: **

Level of exertion: Low to medium

Time for the round: About 3½ hours

Terrain: Mostly on excellent grassy tracks and good paths; the descent from Souther Fell is fairly steep.

The waters flowing from Scales Tarn, cupped in a rocky combe on the east side of the superb mountain of Blencathra, are the principal feeders of the extraordinary River Glenderamackin which, having travelled the first 8 miles/12.8km of its length is still, as the crow flies, only 1½ miles/2.4km from its source. This walk follows its early course.

Park in the hamlet of Mungrisdale, just off the main A66, opposite the Mill Inn or by the phone box (grid ref 362304) just round the corner from it. From this latter point, a public footpath is signed west up a short walled lane, soon becoming an unfenced track beside the River Glenderamackin. The track forks immediately after crossing a subsidiary stream (Bullfell Beck) by a footbridge and it is the left-hand path which now leads alongside the Glenderamackin River. Easy walking follows, including fording the normally very shallow Bannerdale Beck on flat stones, until the virtually treeless valley narrows into a gorge. Here, on White Horse Bent, the river makes its sudden swing to the north-west and the grassy track follows it round, disclosing a most dramatic view ahead of the crags of Sharp Edge rising to Blencathra's summit.

A little track leads down to a footbridge across the Glenderamackin and the popular footpath to Sharp Edge via Mousthwaite Comb will be seen traversing the hillside above; however stay on the north bank until you reach the spoil heap of an old lead mine. Here descend a short slope to cross the now quite tiny stream and join the well-used path up the side of Scales Beck to reach Scales Tarn itself.

If you are capable of it and have the energy, you may circuit the tarn by way of Sharp Edge to Blen-

Sharp Edge seen across Scales Tarn

211

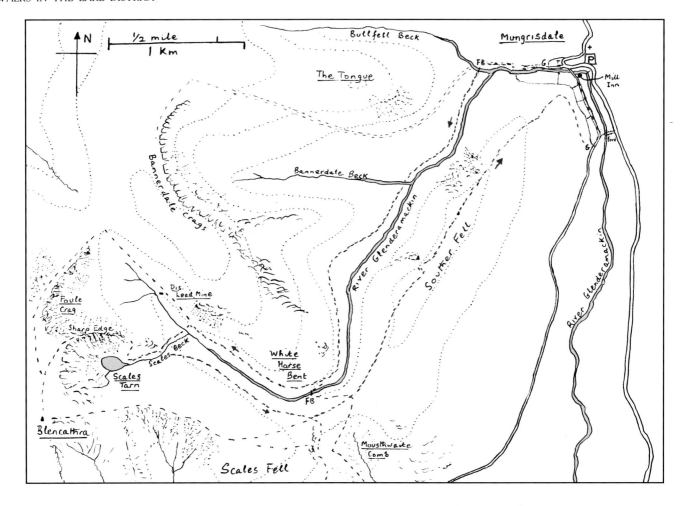

cathra's summit and then descend by Scales Fell. But it is beyond the scope of this book to describe the ascent of Sharp Edge, which curves round the tarn on its north side, for Sharp Edge is not a walk but a serious scramble (i.e. not a rock-climb, but definitely requiring the occasional use of one's hands for balance and for holds). It is quite petrifying to some people, including my wife, although my son, at the fearless age of four, thought it was just a doddle. If it is not for you, enjoy your picnic by the tarn instead.

Leaving the tarn, return alongside Scales Beck and then enjoy the fine traversing path on the south side of the River Glenderamackin as far as the hause at White Horse Bent. Now, when other paths head downhill, yours goes gently uphill to the north-east, onto the broad ridge of Souther Fell. Rising gently over grassy slopes, you by-pass a pillar of stones which must be a beacon as it is not on a summit; the path continues to a real summit cairn and then descends the steepish nose of the fell beyond. At the base of the fell there is, at present, no permitted direct way to the pub through the intake fields, although it is hoped that this may change in the near future. On the final descent, therefore, bear right towards a little stand of larch trees, then continue right alongside the intake wall.

You will very soon reach a metalled road at a gate where a left turn downhill quickly leads to the Mill Inn and the car park again.

Sharp Edge seen from the path near White Horse Bent

59. Mires Beck and Lanty's Tarn from Glenridding

Best Map: OS 1:25 000 Outdoor Leisure 5, North Eastern area

Distance: About 3 miles/4.8km

Highest elevation reached: About 1575ft/480m

Height gained: About 1150ft/350m

Star rating: * *

Level of exertion: Medium

Time for the round: About 2 hours

Terrain: A mixture of stony and grassy paths/

The scenery in the vicinity of Lanty's Tarn, overlooking Ullswater at its southern end, is particularly delightful. You can simply walk up there in half an hour but not get much exercise, so this walk approaches it by way of the Helvellyn path up Mires Beck. That will do your constitution a great deal more good.

There is a large car park in Glenridding (grid ref 385169) at the southern end of the beautiful lake of Ullswater, and some good places for cups of tea and sticky cakes later, when you've earned them, within sight of the car park, so that is a good start. Now leave the car park at the east end, (towards the main road) or use the little snicket (signed 'Helvellyn via Greenside') to reach Greenside Road. This rises westwards between terraced cottages but then forks, the right-hand fork, which you do not want, leading to the old Greenside lead mines; the left hand one turns downhill to the crossing of Glenridding Beck at Rattlebeck Bridge.

Continue past the drive leading into the caravan site and up the walled lane beyond, to the south-west, beside the unruly Mires Beck which clearly floods at times. Ignore the three other paths which turn off to the west and contour towards the old mines at Greenside further up Glenridding Beck, staying on the main uphill one. You shortly cross the Mires Beck to its south bank by a footbridge and then climb grassy slopes towards an apparently distant skyline. Parts of this path are pitched now, large flat stones interlocked to reduce erosion and improve drainage, for it is one of the approaches to Helvellyn, shortly joining the long ridge that sharpens into Striding Edge higher up.

The path reaches this ridge, marked by a solid wall running along its spine, at a broad col; here, where the Helvellyn path turns uphill again, have a little

Looking up Grisedale to Helvellyn from near Lanty's Tarn

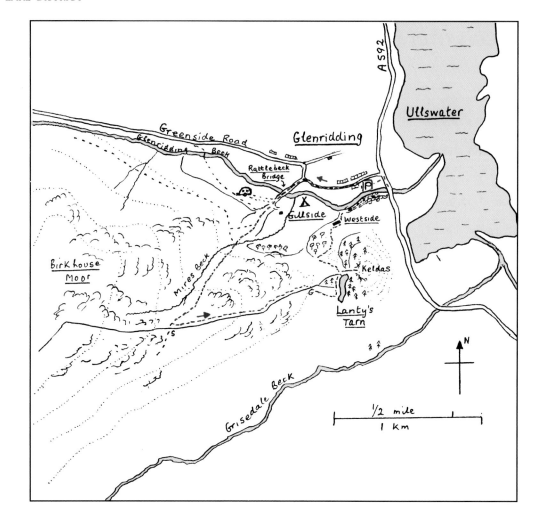

breather and then turn downhill instead. A through-stone stile may be used to cross the wall and gain views up and down Grisedale on its far side but they will become apparent soon enough anyway if you just keep the wall on your right hand and follow a grassy path onto rocky knolls, with grand views down the length of Ullswater. This path gently descends the ridge towards a little wood, with the glint of water seen through the trees; just before reaching the wood, you should turn through a gate in the wall and so reach Lanty's Tarn.

This is a delightful place. The tarn is artificially constructed, with a little dam at its southern end, made up of what are almost two separate pools joined at a narrow neck. It is the surrounding pines and silver birches, however, which give it its especial attraction and will cause you to linger. A gate at the north end of the tarn enables you to turn right and wander up onto the knoll of Keldas. This also has many superb pines and is another wonderful viewpoint, northwards down Ullswater and southwards to St Sunday Crag and Fairfield.

From the gate by the tarn, a well-used and signed path leads north-west in a long slant across grassy fellside (avoiding the old direct route which has suffered badly from erosion) and then slants back north-east above woodland to the cottages at West-side. From here a simple stroll leads down to the main road again and the car park.

Lanty's Tarn, with St Sunday Crag behind

60. Caiston Glen and Red Screes

Best Maps: OS 1:50 000 Landranger 90 Penrith, Keswick & Ambleside area.
At 1:25 000 scale, both Outdoor Leisure 5, North Eastern and 7, South Eastern are needed

Distance: About 4½ miles/7.2km

Highest elevation reached: 2546ft/776m

Height gained: About 1900ft/579m

Star rating: *

Level of exertion: Fairly high

Time for the round: About 3–3½ hours

Terrain: Some rough paths, some open fell; a fairly steep descent from Red Screes, then an easy path to return.

Red Screes tower above the top of the Kirkstone Pass and give a popular ascent from the car park opposite the Kirkstone Pass Inn. However, this walk reaches the top of Red Screes gradually, from the back, so that the fine views from there, when reached, are presented more dramatically. A descent to the pub and a pleasant stroll down an easy path completes it.

There is good parking just south of Caudale Bridge (grid ref 402113). From here you can look directly up the valley of the Caiston Glen, separating High Hartsop Dodd from Middle Dodd and rising to the Scandale Pass, which is where the walk goes. After a hundred paces up the road towards Kirkstone, a finger-post on the right points across fields and then a post with a yellow arrow directs you to a footbridge across the Kirkstone Beck close to its confluence with Caiston Beck.

A ladder-stile over the wall beyond leads up Caiston Glen itself and although the path quickly vanishes, so also does all sight and sound of the traffic on the Kirkstone Pass road. Keeping on the left bank of the stream, whose waters now slide down angled slabs in a dash of white spray, you pass a small spoil heap next to which a solitary rowan marks the old level tunnelling into the fellside. Higher up, the glen opens out into a wide depression and more simple walking leads to the lowest point on the col ahead, the Scandale Pass, where a ladder-stile marks the descent towards Ambleside beyond.

A mostly collapsed wall runs from the pass almost to the top of the Red Screes ridge giving an infallible guide to the path that shadows it uphill. When you meet a transverse wall you know you are nearly at the top and can then slant across the last rise towards the

High wind and snow on the summit of Red Screes with Windermere in the distance

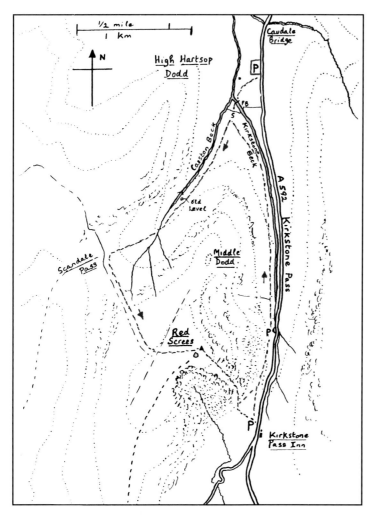

summit, passing one quite small tarn and then a second, larger and almost next to the trig point and nearby cairn. Enjoy, at last, fine views to Helvellyn, to High Street and down to Windermere and, far away, to the sea.

A path leads from the summit windbreak to the south-east and quickly reaches the edge of a deep combe, beyond which the Kirkstone Pass Inn can be seen. The path leads along the left (looking down) edge of the combe, zigzags down broken rocks, turns almost into the combe as the rocks fade into grassy slopes and then easier ground leads down towards the pub, which may provide a welcome stop if you choose.

If you don't, simply swing left (north) before reaching the road and, after a boggy start, shadow the road on a good little path that passes close by the large rock, shaped like a gothic church door, that gives the Kirkstone Pass its name, leading down to the lower car park (grid ref 403089). I recall one winter's day when I was the first person to walk over the pass after a snow storm: there was so much snow and ice that even the snowploughs could not get over and I had to wear crampons on my boots, but the days of hard winters like that seem to have gone.

However, there is no need to walk up or down the road itself nowadays as, just a little lower down, a permissive path is signed. This leads down the left bank of the Kirkstone Beck, giving an easy stroll back to the bottom of the Caiston Glen to connect with the outward path.

Acknowledgements

The author with Henry and Freddie (© Jonathan Allen)

I wish first of all to acknowledge and thank the staff, area managers and rangers of the Lake District National Park who advised me on matters of access on these walks. I also wish to acknowledge my debt to the Ordnance Survey; without their maps I could never have hoped to enjoy so much wonderful walking. My family have yet again endured my irregular hours but have also accompanied me on far, far more of the walks than they did when I was working on either *On High Lakeland Fells* or *On Lower Lakeland Fells*, so perhaps there is a message there. My workaholic editor, Jenny Dereham, whose great help I must acknowledge, does not just check my spellings and punctuation, she also walks over every inch of each walk on the map. Considering that she has done that for all the Wainwright colour-illustrated books as well as mine, she is now a Lake District expert herself. Finally, may I mention my two little canine pals, Henry and Freddie, who accompany me on my days in the hills; I find them a lot more intelligent than sheep.

Index

Addacomb Hole 189
Allen Bank, Grasmere 149
Ambleside 138
Ard Crags 187, 189
Ash Spring Wood 106
Ashness Bridge 161, **165–6**

Bannerdale 207
Barf **183–5**
Barnscar 76
Barrow, near Braithwaite **179–81**
Barrow in Furness 45, 51
Barrowfield, Helsington Barrows 104
Bassenthwaite 185; Lake 199
Beacon Fell, on Blawith Fells **31–2**, 41
Beacon Tarn 32, 41
Beckside, White Combe 49, 51
Beckstones, near Torver 29, **31–2**, 183
Bell, Knott 41; Rib 95, 97; The 25
Bessyboot **171–3**
Birk Field 125
Birks, Bridge 65, 71; house at 54, 71, 73
Bishop, The, painted rock 183
Black Allens bog 67
Black Combe 45, 46, 49, 51, 75, 93
Blake Rigg, above Blea Tarn 15, 17, 54;
    above Tilberthwaite **21–2**
Blawith, Fells 31, 43; Knott **43–4**
Blea, Crag 177; Tarn **15–17**, *17*, **81–3**
Bleak Rigg 189
Blelham Tarn 119
Blencathra 157, 173, 211, 213
Boat How **85–6**
Bolton's Tarn 110

Boon Crag 117
Boot in Eskdale 77, 85, 87
Borrowdale 100, **161–3**, 165, 167, 175;
    Fells 171
Boulder Valley **25–7**
Bowder Stone **167–8**
Bowscale 209; Fell and Tarn **207–9**
Bracken Hause 154
Brackenthwaite Hows **191–3**
Brae Fell 203
Braithwaite 179
Branthwaite 205
Brathay, River 19, 20
Brigsteer 104
Britannia Inn, Elterwater 13, 143
Broadgate 45
Brook House, Dalegarth 85
Broughton in Furness 39, 49
Broughton Mills 53, 55, 61
Broughton Moor Slate Quarry 61
Brown Pike 37, 59
Brown Tongue 95
Buck, Barrow **75–6**, *75*, 99; Crag 71
Bull Haw Moss 37
Burneside 125
Burnmoor Tarn 85, 86
Buttermere valley 187

Caiston Glen **219–20**
Caldew, River 209
Carrock Fell 209
Carron Crag **111–12**
Castle Crag 175
Castlerigg, stone circle 157

Cat, Cove 88; Gill **161–3**, 165, 166
Catbells 173
Caudale Bridge 219
Causey Pike 165, 179
Caw mountain 54, 56, **59–61**
Chapel, Stile 13, 148
Clafhowe Crag 131
Claife Heights, Tarns of **121–2**
Clerk, The, rock 183
Cockhag Plantation 110
Cocklaw Fell 129
Codale Tarn 150
Coniston 25, 115; Old Man 25, 35, 51;
    Water 29, 30, 31, 37, 44
Crag, Hill 179, 187, 189; Wood 120
Croft Head 136
Crofts Head 120
Crook, Crag 93; near Staveley 109
Crummock Water 191, 193, 195, 197
Cumbria Way 11, 32, 177
Cunswick, Fell 105, 106; Scar and Tarn
    105–6

Dalegarth station 81, 83, 85
Dales Way 125, 127
Darling Fell 191, **195–7**
Dead, Crags 199; Pike (Steel Fell) 154
Derwent, River 175
Derwentwater 161, 165, 166
Devoke Water **75–6**, **77–8**, 91
Dodds, the 173, 187, 219
Dore Head, Yewbarrow 95
Dow Crag 35, 45, 91
Dropping Crag 95

Duddon, River 63, 65, 71, 73; Sands 49;
    Valley 36, 53, 54, 55–6, 59, 61, 63, 67
Dungeon Ghyll 13; New Hotel 11
Dunmail Raise, Pass of 153
Dunnerdale 55, *see also* Duddon Valley
Dunnerdale Fells 53

Easedale Tarn **149–50**
Eel, Crag 177, 187; Tarn **87–8**
Elterwater 13, 143; Quarries 13
Ennerdale 76
Esk, River 73, **81–3**, 93
Eskdale 73, 76, 77, 81, 87, 88; Green 76
Esthwaite Water 121

Fairfield Horseshoe 137, 138, 217
Falcon Crags 161, **165–6**
Far Sawrey 121, 122
Fell, Gate 43; Side 205
Fickle Steps **63–5**
Fletcher's Wood **143–4**
Foulsyke 195, 197
Fox Ghyll 137, 138
Foxbield Moss 93
Froswick Fell 131, 138
Froth Pot car park 63, 71
Furness, Abbey 77; fells 43

Gamblesmire Lane 105
Ghyll, Foot 153; Pool 125
Gibson Knott 154
Gilpin, River 109
Glaramara 173
Glen Mary 115

Glenderamackin, River 207, 211, 213
Glenridding, Ullswater 215
Goat Crag 56, 175
Goldrill Hotel, Grasmere 147
Goody Bridge 149, 153
Gowder Dub 175
Grange, Borrowdale 167, 175, 177; Fell 167–8
Grasmere 147, 149, 153; Vale of 147
Grasmoor 195, 197
Great Calva **199–201**
Great Door, Yewbarrow 95
Great Gable 77, 99, 173
Great Langdale **11–13**, *12*, 15, 141, 147
Great Sca Fell, Uldale Fells **203–5**
Great Stickle 53
Great Whinscale 93
Great Wood car park 161, 165, 166
Greatend Crag 167
Greaves Ground 41
Green, Crag **91–3**; Moor 39
Green Quarter Fell 135
Greenburn skyline **153–4**
Greenhead, near Uldale 203
Greenside, Ullswater 215
Greenup Edge 154
Grisedale 217; Pike 179
Grizedale, Forest Park **111–12**
Guards Wood 115, 117

Hag Wood, Great Langdale 11
Hagg Foot 127
Hall Wood, Kentmere 135, 136
Hard Knott, Roman fort 88
Hardknott Pass 91
Hart Howe, near Crook 109
Harter Fell 67, **71–3**, 91
Hartrigg 131
Hawk Rigg **21–2**
Hawkshead 120
Haws Bank 25

Helm Crag 149, 154
Helsington, Barrows 104; Church 103
Helvellyn 187, 215, 220
High Birkhow Wood 99
High Blind How 122
High Fell quarries 21, 22
High Guards 117
High Hall Garth 19
High Moss Tarn 121
High Nest 157
High Raise 173
High Rigg 157
High Spy **175–7**
High Stile 173
High Street 220; fell 131
High Tock How 119
High Tongue 65, 67
High Torver Park 37
Hill Fell 117
Hodge Close Quarries 20
Hodgson's Leap, on Scout Scar 103
Holehouse Tarn 76
Hollin Root 130
Hollow Stones 95
Holme Wood, Loweswater 197
Hugill Fell 135
Hundhowe 127
Huntingstile **147–8**

Ill, Bell 131, 138
Irt, River 100

Keldas knoll 217
Kelly Hall Tarn 8, 29
Kendal 103; Castle 106
Kennel Crag 27
Kent, River **125–7**, 131, 136
Kentmere 129, 131, 135; Head **131–2**; Pike 135; Tarn **135–6**; Valley 125
Kiln Bank, Cross 54; hause 55
King's How **167–8**

Kinmont Buckbarrow 75
Kirk Fell 77, 95
Kirkstile Inn 197
Kirkstone Pass 219, 220
Knott, Hill 45; Rigg **187–9**; The (Duddon Valley) 56
Knottend 45

Lang How 149
Langdale 137, 138; Pikes *12*, *23*
Langstrath 171
Lanthwaite Wood **191–3**
Lanty's Tarn **215–17**
Latterbarrow **119–20**
Levers Water **25–7**
Lily Tarn, on Loughrigg Fell **137–8**
Lingmell 99
Lingmoor Fell 19, 147
'Lion and Lamb' rocks, Helm Crag 154
Little Arrow 35
Little Braithwaite 181
Little Calva, cairn 199, 201
Little Fell **19–20**
Little Langdale **19–20**, 143
Little Loughrigg **141–2**
Little Sca Fell, Uldale 203
Loanthwaite Lane 120
Long Mire Beck **55–6**
Long Moss 167; Tarn 29
Longsleddale 125, **129–30**
Lord's Lot **109–10**
Lord's Seat **183–5**
Loughrigg, Fell **137–8**, **141–2**; Fold 141; Tarn 141
Low Birker 93; Tarn **91–3**
Low Fell, Loweswater 191, **195–7**
Low Fold, near Crook 109, 110
Low Hall Garth 19
Low Rigg **157–9**
Low Wood, near Dalegarth 83
Loweswater 191, 195

Lyth Valley 103

Meadowplatts Plantation 135
Megs Gill **147–8**
Mellbreak 191, 195, 197
Mere, Moss 41; Sike 41
Middlefell 99
Mill Place, Nether Wasdale 99
Miller Brow 138
Mires Beck **215–17**
Miterdale 81
Moment Crag 154
Mosedale 97
Moss Eccles Tarn 121
Mould Rigg 135
Mousthwaite Comb 211
Muncaster, Castle 75, 78; Fell 78
Mungrisdale 207, 209, 211, 213

Naddle Valley **157–9**
Nan Bield Pass 132
Nether Wasdale **99–100**
Newfield Inn, Seathwaite 59, 61
Newlands, Beck **179–81**, 187; Hause 187, 189
Nitting Haws 177

Outgate 119, 120
Overbeck Bridge **95–7**

Park Head Road **55–6**, 61
Pike, of Blisco **15–17**, *15*, *16*; o'Stickle (Langdale) 93; The 93
Pillar 76, 95, 173
Pool Scar 39
Potter Tarn **125–7**
Powter How 183
Prow, The 131
'Pudding Stone', Boulder Valley 25

Quayfoot, car park 167; Quarry 168

Rainsborrow Crag 131
Raven Crag 148
Ravenglass 75, 76
Raven's Crag 56
Red, Pike 95; Screes **219–20**
Rigghead Quarries 175
Rook Howe 131
Rosthwaite 168
Rothay, River 137
Rough Crag 77, 154
Rydal 137

Sadgill, Longsleddale 129
Sail 179, 187; Beck **187–9**; Pass 189
St Catherine's church, Crook 109
St John's in the Vale 159, 201
St Sunday Crag 217
Sawrey Hotel 121, 122
Sawrey's Wood **143–4**
Scafell, Pike 77, 88, 95; Slight Side ridge 77, 85, 88
Scale Bridge 99
Scale Hill Hotel 193
Scales, Fell 211; Tarn **211–13**
Scandale Pass 219
Scar Wood, Cunswick Scar 105
Scout Scar **103–4**, 105
Seascale 100
Seat How 78
Seatallan 95, 97
Seathwaite 59, 61, 67; Tarn 59, **67–9**

Seatoller 171
Sergeant Man 150
Sharp Edge 211, 213
Shepherd Bridge 115
Silver How 147
Silverthwaite car park 141
Siney Tarn **81–3**
Sizergh Castle **103–4**
Skeggles Water **129–30**
Skiddaw 173, 181; Forest 199
Slight Side, Scafell 77, 85, 88
Souther Fell **211–13**
Sprint, River 130
Stable Harvey Moss 32, 41
Stainton Ground Quarries 55
Stainton Pike 76
Staveley 109, 125
Steel Fell **153–4**
Stickle, Pike (Duddon) **53–4**, 55, 93; Tarn 54
Stirrup Crag 95
Stockdale, Longsleddale 129
stone circles, Boot in Eskdale **85–6**; Castlerigg 157; Swinside **45–6**
Stonethwaite 173
Stony Tarn **87–8**
Stoupdale Crags 51
Strands Hotel, Nether Wasdale 99
Styhead Pass 100
Subberthwaite Common 43
Swaledale 205

Swine Crag 49, 51
Swinside, Inn 181; Stone Circle **45–6**

Tarn at Leaves **171–3**
Tarn Beck Seathwaite 59, **63–5**, 67
Tarn Hill **53–4**
Tarn Hows **115–17**
Tarnclose Crag 17, 17
Tewet Tarn 159
Thirlmere 201
Thornthwaite, Swan Hotel 183
Three Shires Inn 19, 143
Tilberthwaite Gill 19, 21
Todd Crag 138
Tongue, The 207
Torver 29, 30, 31, 35, 39; Bottom 35, 37; Commons **29–30**, 31, **35–7**
Tottlebank Height **43–4**
Town End, near Torver 41
Trough House Bridge 83
Troughton Hall Farm 39
Troutal Tongue 67
Troutdale 167

Uldale Fells 203
Ullswater 215, 217
Ulpha 53, 54, 76

Wainwrights Inn, near Elterwater 13
Walla Crag, Borrowdale **161–3**
Walna Scar 37; quarries 59, 61; Road 25, 27, 35, 59

Walney, Isle of 45, 51
Wasdale 77, 95; Fells 86; Hall 99, 100; Head 99
Wastwater 95, 100; Screes 99, 100
Water Crag 77
Whicham Mill 49
Whin Crag 88
Whinlatter 179
White Combe 45, 46, **49–51**
White Horse Bent 211, 213
White Maiden 37, 59
White Pike **59–61**, 76, 78
Whitecombe 49, 51
Whiteside 197; End **135–6**, 191
Whitewater Dash **199–201**
Whitfell 45, 75, 76, 93
Williamson's Monument 135
Windermere 220; Lake 119–20
Wise Een Tarn 121
Woodend Height 76, 78
Woodland Fell **39–41**
Wool Knott **39–41**
Woolpack Inn, Eskdale 87, 91
Wrynose Pass 17

Yew Bank 39
Yew Tree Tarn 115
Yewbarrow **95–7**, 99
Yewdale Fells 115
Yoadcastle 76, 78
Yoke Fell 131